WHAT PEOPL[...]

ZOMBIES O[...] [...]ANJARO

Tim Ward walks up the mountain with his 20-year-old son, and together they explore the power of stories. Amid hallucinogenic walks, bizarre gastronomy, and sing song Tanzanian guides, they illuminate the power and the delusion of the stories we often tell ourselves,and how In letting old stories go, we can find the key to transforming our world.

Carter Roberts, President, World Wildlife Fund US

As with all of Ward's books, it's challenging, exhilarating, brave and profoundly human – I came away from it feeling stimulated, enriched, and also genuinely honoured that an author would take me on such an intensely personal journey. The father-son relationship comes leaping off the page, and the intellectual dimension sizzles and crackles.

Ian Weir, author of *Daniel O'Thunder*

A father-son walk in the clouds. The metaphysical stuff, the meme stuff, I loved it. Really made me think and reflect. I read it like I was eating m&ms or potato chips—compulsively. I think this could have a wide audience. A non-fiction *Sophie's World*.

James O'Reilly, Publisher, Traveler's Tales

In *Zombies on Kilimanjaro*, Tim Ward weaves a healing tale for contemporary men. Part adventure travelogue, part intellectual exploration, part courageous personal revelation, Ward's memoir of climbing the African mountain with his 20-year-old son captivates the reader on multi-levels. *Zombies* tackles the treacherous terrain of fatherhood, philandering, divorce and shadow as Ward demonstrates the healing power of the story well-told. At a time when our culture desperately needs a new definition of the positive masculine, Ward steps up to the plate. Women will also be heartened by his journey on a rugged path that ultimately leads to personal responsibility and adult relationships. I loved it! Its a perfect example of redefining the positive masculine. So honest! So open and vulnerable! So brave! So needed by all the lost men of today. I hope this spawns a whole literary (and other cultural memes) movement.

Marsha Scarborough, author of *Medicine Dance*

My overall impression was one of admiration and enjoyment. I believe you are a father in the truest sense of the word – one who can stumble, try again, err, admit the truth, release and move on. In reality, you are a great dad to Josh, but more importantly you are a great friend to him. Your courage on the physical level was inspiring but your bravery on the emotional level was profoundly moving. You brought us into your family's life and memes, with grace and humility. I was engaged throughout most of the book by your humour and honesty. When you told Josh that he wasn't really him (although it was scary for him) I couldn't stop laughing. The crazy things we parents do! And your scene from a "demented African version of The Sound of Music" was hilarious!

Dee Willock, author, *Falling Into Easy*

Which is harder: climbing the highest freestanding mountain in the world or becoming friends with your adult son from a divorced marriage? In this eight-day tale of courage, conversation, and compassion, Tim Ward does both. His story sounds a rousing call to take responsibility for the natural and social worlds that our children are inheriting from us.

Kimerer LaMothe, author, *Family Planting: A farm-fed philosophy of human relations*

Zombies on Kilimanjaro

A Father-Son Journey
above the Clouds

Zombies on Kilimanjaro

A Father-Son Journey
above the Clouds

Tim Ward

CHANGEMAKERS
BOOKS

Winchester, UK
Washington, USA

First published by Changemakers Books, 2012

Changemakers Books is an imprint of John Hunt Publishing Ltd., Laurel House, Station Approach,
Alresford, Hants, SO24 9JH, UK
office1@o-books.net
www.o-books.com

For distributor details and how to order please visit the 'Ordering' section on our website.

Text copyright: Tim Ward 2011

ISBN: 978 1 78099 339 3

A CIP catalogue record for this book is available from the British Library.

Design: Stuart Davies

Printed in the USA by Edwards Brothers Malloy

We operate a distinctive and ethical publishing philosophy in all
areas of our business, from our global network of authors to
production and worldwide distribution.

CONTENTS

Books by Tim Ward:

What the Buddha Never Taught
The Great Dragon's Fleas
Arousing the Goddess: Sex and Love in the Buddhist Ruins of India
Savage Breast: One Man's Search for the Goddess
The Author's Guide to Publishing and Marketing
(with John Hunt)

For Josh

Acknowledgements

I'm deeply appreciative of the friends and colleagues who read various drafts of this book and gave me helpful feedback. My thanks to Teresa Erickson (my wife), John Hunt, James O'Reilly, Carter Roberts, Paul Rosenberg, Marsha Scarborough, Gordon Thomas, Wendy Ward (my sister), Ian Weir and Dee Willock. Thanks also to my dear friend Wade Davis for his generosity in writing the foreword.

Three other readers deserve special recognition because they truly went the extra mile: Jim Flint volunteered to give my manuscript a thorough and insightful edit. Jennie Sherwin offered to proofread the manuscript and taught me how to use double quotes correctly. Josh Holober-Ward, my son and companion on the trek, read several drafts and helped me accurately portray some of our key conversations. Josh also came up with the book's title.

I would also like to acknowledge the superb team at John Hunt Books and the Changemakers imprint for getting the book so handsomely into print: Maria Barry, Stuart Davies, Mary Flatt, Trevor Greenfield, Catherine Harris, John Hunt, Maria Moloney, Kate Rowlandson, and Nick Welch.

Finally, I'm grateful to Ultimate Kilimanjaro, our tour outfitter (which also provided the maps in this book) and for the crew in Tanzania: Ezekiel, Fred, Sully, Frank, Benjamin, Nathanial, and the rest for providing us such a spectacular experience.

Foreword

by Wade Davis, author, *Into the Silence: The Great War, Mallory, and the Conquest of Everest*

Tim Ward and I have been close friends for more than 20 years and in that time have shared many adventures and misadventures, some on wild rivers and mountain glaciers, others as we've stumbled through the dense and occasionally impenetrable forests of fatherhood. I first knew his son Josh as a lad of six, and recall fondly Tim carrying the boy on his shoulders on a high ridge above the Taku in the remote reaches of northern British Columbia, as the sun set over a herd of caribou on the skyline. Reading Zombies on Kilimanjaro I was pleased to learn that it is now Josh who carries his father up mountains, and in more ways than one.

In this wonderful story of fathers and sons, Tim poises two fundamental and related questions. Why are people drawn to climb the formidable summits of the world, and what is it about the experience that inevitably results in a catharsis of the soul, an opening of the spirit, a softening of the heart? To answer both questions he travels with Josh to the flanks of Kilimanjaro, Africa's highest and most illustrious mountain, a beacon of light rising over an entire continent.

In 1923 while on a speaking tour in New York George Mallory at the end of a lecture was asked why he wanted to climb Everest, no doubt for the umpteenth time. Mallory replied, "Because it's there." This simple retort hit a nerve, and took on an almost metaphysical resonance, as if Mallory had somehow in his wisdom distilled the perfect notion of emptiness and pure purpose. In time, it would be inscribed on memorials, quoted in sermons, cited by princes and presidents. But those who knew Mallory best interpreted it as a flippant response just said to get rid of "a bore who stood between him and a much needed drink." Whatever its genesis the phrase did in fact capture something essential. "Everest is the highest mountain in the world," Mallory later wrote, "Its existence is a challenge. The answer is instinctive, a part, I suppose of man's desire to conquer the universe." Elsewhere he added, "I suppose we go to Mount Everest, granted the opportunity, because - in a word - we can't help it. Or to state the matter rather differently, because we are mountaineers."

Kilimanjaro has this same magnetic appeal to our imagination. But one does not have to be an expert mountaineer like Mallory to climb it. Some 20,000 people reach its summit each year, and so the mountain has become known as Everyman's Everest.

As Tim and Josh make their way to the summit of Kilimanjaro, their conversations grow increasingly breathless as their attention shifts from the personal to the universal. With each step closer to the ice, they become ever more aware of the haunting backdrop of their adventure. First in the most visceral way possible they experience what a climbing friend once told me was the most amazing thing about summiting Everest. The realization that there was a place on Earth where you could get up in the morning, tie on your boots, and under your own power walk in a single day into a zone where the air was so thin that humans could not survive. It was for him a revelation, a completely new perspective on the delicacy of this thin veil of atmosphere that allows life to exist on earth.

Second, as Tim and Josh crest the highest point in Africa they encounter what can only be described as the end of the wild, the melting of the ice and the disappearance of the snows that have for all time given meaning to the mountain. The plight of Kilimanjaro, Tim suggests in some of the most powerful passages in the book, ought surely to serve as a wake up call for all of humanity. The global impacts of climate change are only beginning to be felt. Atmospheric levels of carbon dioxide are at their highest in 650,000 years. Natural habitats everywhere are under threat: coral reefs in the Caribbean, cloud forests of the Andes, the grasslands of the Asian steppe, the lowland rainforests of the Amazon, and the entire arid belt across sub-Saharan Africa.

Arguably the greatest immediate threat is to be found in the mountain ice fields that are the birthplaces of all the world's great rivers. On the Tibetan plateau, source of the Yellow River, the Mekong and Yangtze, the Brahmaputra, Salween, Sutlej, Indus, and Ganges, there has been no net accumulation of snow since at least 1950. Half of humanity depends on these rivers. Throughout the world mountain people who played no role in the creation of this crisis not only are seeing the impact of climate change on their lives, they are taking personal responsibility for the problem, often with a seriousness of intent that puts many of us to shame. In the Andes glaciers are so swiftly receding that pilgrims, believing the mountain gods to be angry, are no longer carrying ice from the sacred mountains back to their communities, forgoing the very gesture of reciprocity that completes the sacred circle of the pilgrimage and allows for everyone to benefit from the grace of the divine.

In Tanzania, the Chagga look up to a mountain that has lost more than 80 percent of its snowcap and ask what will happen to their fields and the very idea of Africa when Kilimanjaro no longer shines over the ancient continent. And this ultimately is the question that Tim ponders in Zombies on Kilimanjaro. Whimsical title aside, it is in fact a profound meditation on the current state of a world in which we as fathers, and mothers, may well be bequeathing to our children a natural world far more impoverished than the one we inherited.

Map courtesy of www.UltimateKilimanjaro.com

Kilimanjaro Trekking Routes. Author's route (Lemosho) as solid white line.

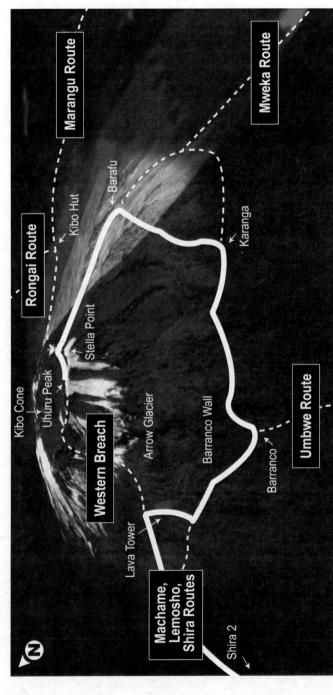

5

Chapter One

Impossible to Climb

Arrival: Moshi, Tanzania

"Your guide will probably tell you," Ezekiel said, "that the name Kilimanjaro comes from *kilima,* the Swahili word for 'mountain,' and *jaro,* the Maasai word for 'white capped.' But that's just for the tourists. We Chagga people who have always lived here, we believe the name comes from our own language: *kilema-kyaro,* which means 'Impossible to Climb.' "

Flying south from Nairobi earlier that day, I had seen Kilimanjaro for the first time. Gazing through the plane window at 17,000 feet in the air, I looked *up* at the peak. Kilimanjaro is the highest point in Africa and at 5,850 meters (19,341 feet) above sea level it's the world's tallest free-standing mountain. I stared at it hard. I have hiked in the Rockies, the Alps, the Himalayas. Yet my mind struggled to fit this solitary, staggering mass of rock into the rest of the landscape: a glacier-ringed mountain at the equator; a rainforest in the middle of a desert.

From the Serengeti plains to the Indian Ocean, East Africa is mostly yellow sand and red clay. But from the white-streaked crown of Kilimanjaro's volcanic cone run streams and springs that trickle down through miles of grey lava and scree to create a green girdle of rainforest in the foothills. A vast, flowing skirt of cultivated, fertile land encircles the mountain for hundreds of square kilometers below. As if by some mysterious power, the mountain makes its own weather. It conjures clouds from the hot air, bringing down rain and dew that nourishes the land even during the long, arid months when the surrounding savannah turns as dry as bones.

"It's like walking from the equator to the North Pole in a week," Ezekiel told me.

The two of us sipped sweet milk tea at a stall outside Kilimanjaro Airport. Ezekiel was a young Tanzanian man with dark black skin. He wore a red t-shirt with *SPAIN* written on it in big yellow letters, the team he was cheering for in the 2010 World Cup. Ezekiel worked for the company we hired for our trek up the mountain and he had met me in the terminal when my plane landed. Now he was keeping me company while I waited for my son Joshua's flight to arrive from the US.

"So do you work in Nairobi?" Ezekiel asked.

"I was only in Kenya for ten days, working for the World Bank. My wife Teresa and I run a small communications consulting company. We work for development and environmental organizations. The two of us train their experts all over the world to communicate better about why their projects and programs make a difference. Things such as why it's important for local banks to finance small businesses, and how to get electricity into remote villages."

"And where is your wife?"

"Teresa had to return home to Washington DC to spend time with her daughter. I stayed in order to climb Kilimanjaro with my son, Josh. He just finished his first year at college. He's studying to be an actor at the University of Maryland."

"He's a movie star?"

"Not yet, but it wouldn't surprise me someday. He has been on an American national TV show, and in a lot of plays."

"He's handsome then?"

"Hey, I'm his father. Of course I think he's handsome. Friends tell me he looks like a young John Cusack." From Ezekiel's blank stare, I could tell this description meant nothing. "Well, let's just say he's got a lot more hair on his head than his old man," I added.

"So it is just the two of you climbing, father and son?"

"Yes, that's the idea," I nodded. "I haven't seen much of him in the last few years. We used to do a lot of wilderness vacations together. When he was younger, before he started doing theater camps every summer, we would go river rafting in Western Canada and sea kayaking. We even did a safari in South Africa when he was thirteen, and we got chased by a rhino. It's been six or seven years now since we've done something like this–well, I guess we've never done anything quite like Kilimanjaro."

We heard a distant roar in the sky. Josh's KLM flight was headed for the runway. When the plane touched down, I talked the customs officers into letting me back into the baggage claim area. From there I could peer through the immigration lanes, spot him, and let him see that I was waiting for him. A minute later I recognized the unruly head of thick brown hair bopping through the gate and into the building. He was one of the first off the packed flight. We waved wildly at each other. When I see Josh after several weeks apart, it's still sometimes a shock. How did that little kid I used to pick up by an arm and a leg and twirl around while he made airplane noises turn into this lumbering twenty-year-old with sideburns and stubble who wears the same-sized clothes as me? He may seem like a man on the outside, but I still see all the behaviors he had when he was a child–the way his right foot sometimes drags just a fraction, how he bites the inside of his cheeks when he's distracted, that puppy-dog smile of unbridled affection. I see all these things and it sometimes creates the illusion for me that he's still a little boy wearing a Halloween man-suit.

I gestured to Josh that he needed to fill out a form to get his entry visa. I knew if he could do this quickly he could beat the rush. 350 tourists were filing out of the plane right behind him. He found the form then knelt on the floor, his legs splayed out in an M-shaped position as he filled in the boxes. No, no, I gestured frantically, not on the floor! Get in line and do it, otherwise the queue will fill up and it will take forever! But his head was drooped down, concentrating on the paper. The place was now too noisy for me to be heard even if I yelled. I watched, helpless, waiting for him to look up, willing him to look up. God, just chill, I told myself. He's been on his own in college for a year. He can navigate his own way through a border crossing. So what if it takes an extra hour?

The luggage carousel started up. I know, I'll wait for his bag, I told myself. For 45 minutes I watched four hundred rucksacks and gear bags spin round and round, searching for Josh's new blue duffel among them. We had bought it together in the spring at REI, and stuffed it full with new boots, shirts, thermal underwear, fleece, and a poly-fill jacket. I remembered my own first duffel bag stuffed with similar gear–but for work, not play. I was seventeen and headed for Saskatchewan to live in a tent and sweat twelve hours a day under the hot prairie sun on a pipeline survey crew. By Josh's age I had spent over a year of my life in various survey crews and oil rigs to make money for college. I watched the luggage go round and round, and remembered what it was like to be young, strong, and living outdoors.

It was hard at first for a nerdy, middle-class kid like me to do punishing, physical labor and fit in with the tough bastards who work on pipelines and oil rigs. But my dad had done the same thing when he was a young man. He had worked as a deckhand on Lake Ontario and cut brush for new power lines in Northern Ontario. He helped me get my first jobs out west. I remember figuring it out that for many generations boys my age went off to war, and the ones who survived came back as men. I knew I was lucky there were no wars when I was growing up. But I also knew I needed some kind of rite of passage. The oil rigs did it for me. There were days that I cried in my bunk, scared and exhausted, knowing that no one within two thousand miles cared if I lived or died. But I kept pulling on my boots and hardhat. Not a war hero. But by surviving I knew I could make it in the world of men. It changed my perception of who I was.

I remembered coming back from the rigs before starting university in the summer of 1978. My dad took one look at me, squeezed my large bicep then challenged me to arm wrestle. I tried to put him off, but he insisted. He had beaten me at this game more times than I could tell when I was a teen. We went out to the back patio and sat down on either side of the table. I beat him slowly with my right hand, then quickly with my left. That was last time we ever played that particular game together.

"Hey, Dad!" Josh bounded through immigration.

He threw his arms round me and squeezed. Josh has this great, uninhibited, full-body grab. When my own father hugged me, I used to flinch. Right up into my late forties I had to steel myself for his embrace. He'd spanked us as kids, and told us that love meant teaching us discipline. Decades later I still had to fight a reflex to pull back when he touched me. That's part of why I never hit Josh, and I'm grateful to my ex-wife that despite all our fights, on this issue we agreed. As a little kid Josh would sling his arms around my neck and just hang on me. I'd feel him breathe deep and relax. I loved this sense of being a safe place for him, a shelter. That had changed some as he grew older, especially during his teenage years, when he and I had fought and there had been a time there was a real fracture in our relationship. That was past now, but the memory of those childhood hugs came back to me at moments like this.

"Good flight?" I asked as we walked back to the baggage carousel.

"Yeah, great, especially the part from Amsterdam. I was in the security line at the gate, and the guard was giving this Dutch family ahead of me a real hassle because they had one bag too many. It was just a small bag of candies and stuff, but they were really overloaded with kid stuff. They had these two cute little girls, just adorable and blonde, you know, pigtails and all. So I said, 'Hey, let me take the bag through, no problem.' The family ended up sitting near me on the plane and the girls fed me chocolates all through the flight."

I grinned and choked back the urge to blurt out: 'Never, never, never, never carry a bag through airport security that belongs to someone else!' Instead, I told him the story of how his mother and I had once mailed a package for a friendly young couple we met at a youth hostel when traveling in Tibet:

"…And when we got back from the post office, where we had signed all the customs forms, the couple asked us how it went. No problem, we said. Then they told us the parcel contained hashish they were smuggling home. Your mom and I could easily have spent several years in a Chinese prison for that small good deed, had a postal worker decided to inspect."

"Holy shit, Dad. But come on, it's not the same at all. This was a bag of candy for some little blonde Dutch girls, not miniature drug dealers."

"You don't know, Josh, you don't know. From Amsterdam, who knows what they are packing?"

"So," Josh interrupted, "before even touching down in Africa, I've taken someone else's bag onto an airplane *and* I took candy from strangers. I'd say I'm off to a good start getting used to the dangers of Kilimanjaro! Hey–there's my bag!"

His blue duffel bag slid towards us on the carousel. Josh grabbed it and we headed past customs to where Ezekiel stood waiting.

"Hey Joshua!" he said, reaching out a large, black hand.

He shook Josh's hand with a complex three-grab motion: clasp wrists, handshake, then clasp fingers. I had flubbed the maneuver when Ezekiel first greeted me, but Josh caught on easily enough. Ezekiel grinned, grabbed his bag, and loaded us onto the bus.

One thing I admired about my son was his great natural timing. He could have stressed and made it through the visa lines first and waited for an hour. Instead, he waltzes out and his bag arrives as if on cue. He's a classic Type B' personality, relaxed and easy going. Me, I'm Type A. I'm more inclined to grab life by the horns and grapple with it. Sure, I think life is an adventure. But after thirty-five years of work, travel and parenting, I've learned to keep my bearings, watch for landmarks, pack the wet-wipes, and never ever leave my bag unattended. With Josh, however, I often feel like the grandfather in the *Peter and the Wolf* tape we used to listen to when he was a kid. Cue the bassoon: "But what if a wolf *did* come out of the forest? What if there had been drugs in the candy bag? What then!?"

It had been easy enough to get along with Josh while he was off at college. I saw him once a month or so when he came back to stay at his mother's house for the weekend. But now we were going to be together for eleven days and nights, including seven on the mountain. We weren't even out of the airport and already I was struggling to stay out of lecturing-parent mode. As we settled into our seats on the bus, I thought again of my own father. I had chosen to go to university three thousand miles away from home in part because I needed to get away from his domineering personality.

There are many ancient myths in which the young hero kills or wounds his father in order to take the throne, throw off the old order, or overcome the Dark Side of the Force. Cronus, Zeus, Oedipus, Luke Skywalker: each mark out an archetypal struggle that is true for all sons and fathers in some way or other. Josh took his own turn at this when he was 17. Less than a month into his senior year of high school he and I were fighting over homework assignments that he had been blowing off yet again. It drove me crazy. I kept trying to make him do it, and he'd just lie to me or make up some excuse. Sure, he wasn't doing drugs or stealing cars, so I figured a little bit of butting heads was probably healthy, and I didn't mind being the bad cop, even though it aggravated me. I was yelling, about to ground him again, when he suddenly said to me:

"I don't have to put up with this. I can go and live full time with my mom."

Since the divorce, when Josh was only three, he had been living half the time with his mother, the other half with me. As an author and consultant, I had structured my life to be a full-time parent during my weeks with Josh. With a single stroke he ended that arrangement. He packed up his stuff and his mother drove over to my house to pick him up. I was furious, as much at her as at him. For the next six months Josh refused to see me, even at Christmas. When at last he broke the ice the following spring, we met for a milkshake at the Tastee Diner where we used to hang out. We talked about what happened between us, but he and I had very different memories about what led to our rift, so we just let it rest. He then told me he was going to keep living with his mother full time, but wanted to see me too.

With restraint I replied, "What's past is past. So let's use what happened between us to start a new relationship, man to man..."

Since that day, almost three years earlier, he and I had pretty much patched things up. But I felt a distance between us that had not existed before. True to his word, Josh never spent a night at my house again. The cord had been cut.

We rolled through the warm African night towards the town of Moshi, where we would sleep before beginning our climb the next morning. I asked Josh about his plans for the rest of the summer.

"I'll hang out with Andrew for a while at his mom's house in Baltimore. He and I are going to be quad-mates at school next year with two other guys. It's going to be great living in an apartment on campus with friends, instead of a dorm. Not that the dorm was bad. But my old roommate liked to drink beer and smoke pot. I mean, I drank the occasional beer with him, but I never even liked the smell of pot. One of the things I like about the guys I'm going to be living with is that we all agreed this was not going to be a party house. And between the four of us we've got some great gaming equipment...Then later in the summer

I'm going to fly out and visit Susie in her new place near Seattle."

Susie was his girlfriend, who had moved to Washington State at the end of the last semester.

"So, what about that pirate job?" I asked.

Josh had applied for a job working for a kiddie cruise line out of Baltimore harbor, a summer camp on board a pirate ship, where the crew-counselors dressed in costume and stayed in character. He had been telling pirate jokes and practicing his accent for about a month in preparation for the job interview, as in: "Why can't little kids watch *Pirates of the Caribbean*? Because it's rated *Arrrr*."

"I didn't get the job," he shrugged. "But that's okay. I need a break anyway."

"What? From the rigors of acting school?" I blurted out.

"Yeah," he said, oblivious to my sarcasm. "So I'm just as glad I don't have to work this summer."

We lapsed into silence. I looked out the window. Josh seemed to be wired so differently than I was at his age, with my need to prove myself, earn my place in the world of men. I worried sometimes that he had missed out on the rites of manhood. The path my dad and I had taken, doing physically punishing work, is a toughening process. It seemed to me Josh wasn't getting this. Everything seemed to come to him too easily. Like me, Josh took a gap year after high school. But instead of heading into the wilderness to work in a camp and save for college, he enrolled in massage school and got his professional license. He told me that as a young actor, a day job as a masseur would be better than waiting tables because you could see clients during the mornings and do shows in the evening. It made sense, but I didn't see how that would pay for college. Years ago I had promised I would pay half his college fees (having set up a college fund for this purpose when he nine). It was a lot more expensive than when I was his age, so I figured fifty percent would give him incentive to earn the rest. But he didn't seem to be thinking about it at all. Then midway through his gap year, he applied for and won an acting scholarship that covered about 85 percent of his total college costs for four years.

"You should thank me, Dad, for all the money I saved you," he told me when he shared the good news.

I was happy for him, happy for me, too, having to write checks for only a few thousand dollars per year. When school started he set up an on-campus massage service, earning enough to cover all his running expenses so he didn't have to ask for money along the way. So he was on the road to independence. Easy for him, easy for me. Yet something about our arrangement left me feeling jangly and unsatisfied. I guess just wanted to see him struggle for it more.

"So, how'd work go in Nairobi?" Josh asked, snapping me out of my thoughts.

"Good, good. Most of the people we trained were Africans working for the private sector arm of the World Bank called IFC. They work with businesses and regulators to help create jobs and deliver services to poor people. For example one of the women in our course is part of a Lighting Africa initiative that promotes low-cost ways of getting light to poor villages that are far from the electricity grids. They have competitions for the best ideas, and then help the winners get their lights to market. One winner is a device you stick in the ground that takes advantage of the slight conductivity of soil microbes to generate an electric current. Another is a solar-powered LED light you can put in front of your home to charge during the day, then bring inside at night, so kids can study for school, or adults can work. This clean technology also reduces the pollution, health and safety problems caused by kerosene lamps."

"Cool."

"We also got to learn about some of the really tough problems in East Africa, the sort of things you might not think about at all in North America. For instance, another of our participants is working on changing regulations for land ownership in Kenya. She told us that right now, about 50 percent of the households in Kenya are headed by women. A lot of this is because of AIDS. But women own only about one percent of the property in the whole country. Property laws reflect this deep inequality of Kenyan society. Because these women often don't own the land they and their families are living on, they have no collateral to get loans to start businesses. They don't even have much incentive to improve their properties or farmland, because male relatives have the power to take it away. So if you are going to help people bring themselves out of poverty, you have to have laws in place that make it possible. Our job is to help these World Bank experts, who are very dedicated, very bright people, convince the public and government that it needs to be done. Frankly, people in these big development institutions are not very good at communicating. They have all this amazing technical expertise, but it's hard for them to boil it down in simple terms so ordinary people can get it."

"Well, that sucks."

"Yeah, but it does keep Teresa and me in business."

"So, what's next?"

"Well, we've got some work in India and the Philippines coming up in the fall. But for me the real challenge of the next few months is going to be distilling what I've been researching on meme theory into new course modules that we can teach. I'm really glad you've agreed to help me out with this."

"No problem."

Josh had agreed to be my sounding board as I tried to figure out how to make meme theory comprehensible. For over a year I had been fascinated with this new understanding of how ideas spread and evolve. I wanted to use this theory in our communications training courses. The problem I faced was that books on the subject seemed stuck in the same kind of dense, technical jargon that makes the World Bank's work so tough to comprehend. Indeed, every time I tried to explain meme theory to others, their eyes glazed over. So, since Josh and I were going to have so much time together on the mountain, I figured this would be a great opportunity to go through the theory with him to see if I could talk about memes in terms that made sense and seemed relevant to a college student.

"What can't the two of you just climb the mountain together?" Teresa asked when I told her about my plan just before she and I parted in Nairobi. "Why does there have to be some kind of agenda?"

"I thought it would give us something to talk about on the long walk," I replied defensively. "It'll be fun."

"Fun?" She looked at me with that who-do-you-think-you-are-kidding expression in her brown eyes. "It sounds more like you are trying to lure Josh into some kind of Socratic-dialogue-transmission-of-wisdom thing while you've got him captive."

"Okay," I admitted, "sometimes I find it hard to talk to Josh. I'm fine with the superficial conversations. How's school, what's happening at work, opinions about movies and shows. But I feel awkward a lot of the time, like I don't really know what to say to him. I want to be able to talk about the things that are really interesting to me, too. I thought my plan would be a great way to give our conversation some structure, some depth…"

"You hear how weird that is?"

"No."

Teresa shook her head and put a hand on my arm.

"Tim," she said gently, "You think you're all better from the trauma you felt when Josh left you to live with his mom. But I think you're not yet healed. On the surface, things seem fine. And for Josh, they probably are. He did what he needed to do, separating from you. But I notice you still seem tentative around your son, as if something you might do or say could break a bond that to you still seems fragile."

Sitting next to me on the bus, Josh had fallen asleep. His head leaned against my shoulder. I smiled. Remembering Teresa's words, I thought about what kind of a relationship Josh and I would have in the years ahead as he grew into a man. I found myself appreciating what it must have been like for my own father when I left home in my twenties, not returning at times for two years at a stretch. I had spent six years in Asia, and twenty more years in the US. I spoke about once a week with my parents by phone, and I tried to visit them in Ottawa twice every year. Suddenly I saw the father-killing myths from the deposed dad's point of view. Even if Darth Vader couldn't turn Luke to the Dark Side, I'm sure he still wanted to be part of his son's life in a more than tangential way. But what does a parent have to offer when the parenting is done? Yes, we want our kids to be independent. But we also want them to stay connected, stay intimate. We don't want them to drift away altogether.

At heart I suppose I hoped climbing Kilimanjaro might put Josh and me on a clearer path to that man-to-man relationship I had said I wanted after our split. But there's a risk, isn't there, in seeking an adult relationship with your grown-up kid? When you are a parent, your children know you as "Dad" or "Mom" and that's all that you are to them. There are things about ourselves we parents choose to keep from our kids. We tell ourselves it's for their own good. That's wise, no doubt. But if you are going to have an adult relationship, that's got to change. I thought again of Darth Vader (the name itself a clever play on Dark Father). Dying in Luke Skywalker's arms, Vader asks his son to remove the black mask and helmet so that he can see Luke with his own eyes—and in the process, reveal his scarred and damaged face to his son. I wanted that kind of authenticity with Josh, but I had to admit, I did not know how to get there from here.

In North America when we think of Africa most often we think of gorillas in the mist, wildebeests sweeping across the plains, or else grueling poverty, AIDS orphans, and bloody, violent civil wars in places like Rwanda, Congo, Zimbabwe, Sierra Leone and Sudan. We don't think of Moshi, a bustling town of concrete and glass buildings at the heart of a thriving tourist industry. It has markets, banks, ATMs, pharmacies, souvenir shops and travel agencies. In truth, there are countless towns like this across Africa, as the continent's steady economic growth over the past decade has begun to create a decent life for millions of people.

We drove through the lit streets of downtown Moshi and then down a dark and quiet road to the Springlands Hotel. Inside the high yellow wall we found a courtyard garden filled with palm trees. Meandering brick walkways led through the garden to covered tables, an outdoor bar, a large, blue, chlorinated swimming pool, an Internet café, and an outdoor restaurant. A crowd of mostly European tourists gathered in the TV room, watching highlights of the latest World Cup match, the final now just eight days away. The temperature was pleasant, neither hot nor cool, and the air was still. I noticed there were no mosquitoes. Though malaria is a problem in this part of Tanzania, in the dry season there's not a lot of water lying around, so mosquitoes don't breed.

Ezekiel waved goodbye to Josh and me, instructing us to meet him in the courtyard at 8 a.m. the following morning for our final briefing. He told us we could rent any gear we needed right at the hotel, including sleeping bags, walking poles, and winter coats. He also said to repack our bags with only 15 kilos (33 pounds), including all our gear, as that was the legal limit the porters were allowed to carry. He pointed out a metal hook suspended from a metal frame with a scale attached, so we could weigh our bags to make sure we were not over the allotted weight. The excess baggage we could store in the luggage room till we returned. Our passports, credit cards and any other valuables could be left in one of the hotel's safety-deposit boxes. I appreciated the well thought-out efficiency of the whole operation.

The room was Spartan but clean, with three cot-like beds, mosquito nets, a row of shelves, and a clean private bathroom with abundant hot water–a luxury I knew we would soon leave behind. Neither of us had eaten for several hours, but the restaurant was closed. The gift shop, however, was open. I bought water, a package of chocolate biscuits, and two Kilimanjaro guidebooks. Back in the room we munched biscuits and sorted through our stuff. I had known about the weight limit, but had not counted on that including our sleeping bags. We evaluated every item, trying to decide what was essential and what to leave behind.

Exhausted, Josh slept.

I picked up the guidebooks and started to read.

The first recorded reference to a "great snow mountain" in Africa comes from the Greek mapmaker, Ptolemy, in the 2nd Century A.D. Sixteen centuries later, rumors of a mountain "topped with silver" spread from slave traders on the East Africa coast to Europeans. The first European to explore the mountain's bottom slopes, a German missionary named Johannes Rebmann, recognized that silver as snow. But when in 1849 he reported an ice-cap on the equator to his geographic society back home, the experts declared this was impossible. They concluded that Rebmann must have been suffering from malaria-induced hallucinations. Once Europeans established the mountain was not just a myth, they immediately set about trying to conquer it, only to be turned back again and again by steep walls of ice covering the top two kilometers of its cone. The peak was not summited until 1889–with a second ascent only succeeding twenty years later. Britain and Germany fought through World War One for control of Kilimanjaro's green valleys, and then after the Second World War the impossible-yet-real mountain became a symbol of Africans' dream of freedom from colonial rule. In 1961, newly independent Tanganyika placed a torch on the summit, which

President Julius Nyerere declared a "beacon of freedom" for the rest of Africa.

Ernest Hemingway's 1936 short story, *The Snows of Kilimanjaro* (also available at the Kilimanjaro gift shop) made the mountain famous throughout the Western world. Hemingway described flying in a small plane towards the peak, "wide as all the world, great, high, and unbelievably white in the sun." But this vision of Kilimanjaro was not the same mountain I had seen earlier that day as I flew in on my own small plane. Today Kilimanjaro is mostly grey at the peak, with streaks and splotches of white that look as if the mountain is wearing not a crown of ice, but a fractured tiara. In fact, in the past hundred years close to 90% of its permanent ice has disappeared.

Al Gore showed pictures of Kilimanjaro's vanishing glaciers in *An Inconvenient Truth*. The shocking loss of ice in photos from 1970 and 2000 turned the iconic mountain into a geological poster child for Climate Change. Although rapidly retreating glaciers have been documented all over the world, Gore's choice of Kilimanjaro created great controversy. Skeptics pointed out that Kilimanjaro's ice fields have been shrinking for at least a hundred years, whereas the rise in global temperatures attributed to Climate Change only began in the 1980s. As a result, each new scientific study of this remote peak becomes the focus of furious debate: Are Kilimanjaro's dying glaciers a harbinger of a human-caused catastrophe that we could still avert? Or are they the result of natural processes beyond our control? Regardless of the cause, scientists agree that within the next twenty years, the last of the glaciers will have disappeared from Kilimanjaro.

With the melting of the ice, the mountain formerly known as "Impossible to Climb" has turned into a relatively easy trek, at least in terms of technical ascent. About 40,000 people make the attempt each year. But only an estimated forty to fifty percent make it all the way to the top. The guidebooks are all rather vague about the actual number. The reason so many trekkers don't make the peak is Acute Mountain Sickness (AMS), commonly called altitude sickness. At the summit, air pressure is so low there is only half as much oxygen as at sea level. It's like living in a partial vacuum. The sickness hits people in different ways, most often with headaches, nausea, vomiting, insomnia, disorientation and exhaustion. One weird symptom I experienced a few times in the Himalayas was euphoria. High altitude makes me high. I want to run and jump and fly and everything seems really, really funny. This is not very helpful frame of mind when you are scaling a mountain top.

In the worst cases AMS turns into two conditions that can quickly kill you. With High Altitude Pulmonary Edema, fluid seeps into your lungs so swiftly you literally drown in your own juices. With High Altitude Cerebral Edema, fluid leaks into your brain. This affects your balance, your memory, and can even put you in a coma. The websites say that on average ten trekkers die each year on Kilimanjaro–most from altitude sickness, and a few due to rockslides. (No statistics exist on the numbers of porters and guides who perish). Ten deaths in 40,000 is only .025 percent. If it were a batting average, it would be a 99.975 percent survival rate. Not bad odds, I figured. But what makes altitude sickness particularly tricky is that you never know who is going to get it. You can be young and fit and it might kill you. Or you can be old out of shape, just shuffling along, and you'll be fine. In fact, the oldest person up Kilimanjaro was an 87 year old Frenchman, while tennis champion Martina Navratilova had to abandon her climb when AMS hit her hard.

What precautions to take? Some websites recommend four-to-six weeks of intensive training, bringing altitude-sickness pills, oxygen bottles, and a portable hypobaric chamber. Blogs from some victorious climbers scoffed at all this. In the end I decided to follow the 'travel light' recommendation offered by Ultimate Kilimanjaro, the trekking company whose online photos and snappy prose had the attitude I liked best and decided to book with. I chose not to worry about emergency equipment, trusting that our guides would know what they were doing.

"You know Dad, it seems it's not a vacation with you unless there's a chance we'll die," Josh said to me while discussing AMS before the trip.

"Hmm. I guess that's true," I replied. "But it's that risk that makes a vacation an adventure!"

"Who do I remind you of?" my father said to Teresa within five minutes of meeting her for the first time.

He stroked his short brown beard, flecked with grey. Teresa threw me a glance asking for help.

"Hemingway," I said tersely.

"Oh yes," Teresa said, "you look just like Hemingway."

"That's right!" My father grinned. "Everywhere I go people tell me I look like Hemingway."

As a journalist, my father had covered wars in Cyprus and Viet Nam, gone on press tours of Taiwan, Cuba, Iran, and behind the Iron Curtain. When he visited Spain, he made a point to watch a bullfight. He had a sailboat on the Ottawa River, and he wore a captain's hat. Charismatic and intelligent, overbearing and loquacious, he used to hold forth at the family dinner table about politics, economics and global affairs. Competitive, he hated to surrender a point in any argument. He had boxed when he was in school. He never let any of us win, even at simple board games. Every victory was hard-won. When I was a teen, he used to beat me regularly at chess, and when I started beating him, he said: "When your son defeats you, you never really lose." He said it as if turning my victory into a feat of one-upmanship for him.

When he would introduce me to strangers, he would sometimes say "This is my boy, Tim" and I would rankle at his possessive use of that small word. When I finished high school, he wanted me to go to the military college where he had gone. Instead I went to university three thousand miles away and majored in philosophy. When I came home for Christmas, armed with rationalism and logic, I would challenge his premises across the dining room table, and call him on his faulty inferences.

"Now I know why they made Socrates drink hemlock," he told me.

Yes, to me he seemed just like Hemingway, and I was so damn clear that I was not going to grow up to be like him.

He also told me that he loved me, often and with affection. He would describe in teary detail how he felt when he first held the bloody bundle that was me on the day I was born. His sentimentality drove me nuts. I loved him and I wanted to get away from him, to create a safe buffer and live my life on my own terms.

I grew a beard like him when I turned 18. I felt it made me look like a man. I worked in the bush like him to pay my way, and after college I left to travel the world, living in India and China and Japan, working as a journalist like him. In my thirties, he invited me to join him in his media consulting business. He retired a decade ago, and that's the company Teresa and I now own. She tells me in the training room I have many of his gestures and mannerisms, and that I cling stubbornly to his way of doing things.

And like my father, when I held my son in my arms for the first time and looked deep into his eyes, I knew I would do everything in my power to nurture and protect this little boy.

Chapter Two

In the Cloud Forest

Day 1: to Big Tree Camp (2,895 meters)
3 kilometers

Duffle bags weighed and packed, Josh and I sat with ten other trekkers around one of the garden tables while Ezekiel briefed us. All of us were headed for the Lemosho Route, one of the longer and less-traveled paths up the mountain. Though we were part of different groups, we would all be spending the first day together riding the bus and then walking to the first camp. Our group consisted of four silver-haired New Zealanders, three Canadians (Josh, myself, and a teacher from northern Quebec named Mike), a middle-aged Scottish couple, a young German couple, and a wiry young Aussie named Bryce.

"The golden rule of the mountain is, 'Slowly, slowly,' " Ezekiel warned in a voice both friendly and stern. "You follow the instructions of your guides. It's their job to help you get to the top. You don't rush. You let them set the pace. If you have trouble breathing, or headache or you feel like vomiting, anything, you tell them. When you are climbing to the summit, if they tell you to go down, you do as they say. You have to remember that high altitude can be very dangerous. So your guide is like your guardian angel. His most important job is to get you safely back to your loved ones."

The meeting closed with us all signing a set of forms attesting that we had emergency evacuation insurance and releasing the company from any liability from injury or death. Ezekiel then loaded us onto a grimy minibus. The bus had plush foam seats with cigarette burns in them. In one place a chunk was torn out of the padding as if an animal had chewed off a corner. We took our seats and waved goodbye to Ezekiel and the comforts of the Springlands Hotel.

The landscape changed dramatically as we left Moshi's paved streets. At first we passed concrete buildings, crowded streets, tin roofed kiosks, hawkers selling Afro-kitsch carvings and made-in-China t-shirts with zebras and lions on them. The air stank of diesel exhaust that belched black clouds from the rear ends of trucks and overcrowded minibuses. At the outskirts of town we passed fields of dried maize, potatoes, and further on, rows and rows of coffee bushes–a major cash crop. Asphalt disappeared. Red dust from the dirt track spooled up from our wheels leaving behind clouds that turned the shrubs on the roadside the color of dried blood. The buildings devolved from cement office blocks to single-story shops, then rudimentary shacks. Concrete cinderblocks gave way to wooden walls and tin roofs were replaced with thatch. Donkeys pulling carts appeared instead of trucks and some of these carts even had wooden wheels. When we reached the foothills we saw villagers chopping clods of hard dirt with hand hoes, turning the red soil for planting. Men and women balanced loads of fuel wood on their heads, or carried white sacks of potatoes as they trudged from the fields back to their villages.

A troop of baboons wandered along the opposite side of the road, oblivious to the humans.

"Look at that!" said Vanessa, the Scottish woman, who was sitting on one side of me. "Just two primate species sharing a common path!"

The previous week in Kenya I learned that fossil hunters in search of early humans in the famed Rift Valley look for baboon bones, because the two species are so often found in the same locations. We are both intelligent, adaptable creatures who evolved in the same African landscapes. We both lived in groups of 50-200. We form lifelong bonds between individuals, and create social alliances and hierarchies. A million years ago, there was probably not that much difference between us. Then in just a blip in the evolutionary timescale, something radical happened that knocked us off that common path. It was this radical thing that changed our destiny that excited me most about meme theory.

Vanessa pointed to the women working with hoes in the potato field. She told me it reminded her of a BBC reality TV show called *Tribal Wives*. Each episode a British woman goes and lives in a different tribal society.

"The hardest thing for these women was the sheer physical demand of tribal life," she said. "The repetitive tasks like planting rice. It's so hard for us in the West to do this kind of work."

"I remember this from my own travels in Asia," I replied. "Sometimes I would spend a day working in the fields. The physical part was hard, yes, but the mental part was worse. I would look at the vast swaths of land ahead of us and think, 'My God, how will we ever finish?' My back would start to ache and I worried about how much more it would hurt by lunchtime. Everyone else just sang harvests songs and chatted while they worked. They thought it was hilarious that I wanted to finish quickly. We in the West live in this rush towards the future, like we're always trying to meet a deadline. We treat time like a scarce commodity. As a result, it seems like there's never enough of it."

"People who live on the land like that don't share our modern sense of time," Vanessa replied thoughtfully. "For them time is seasonal, looping. The time of harvest and of planting, they come back year after year. So there's always plenty of time, enough for everything."

I enjoyed Vanessa's warmth and engagement. She was blonde with a roundish face. Like me, she was in her early fifties. Her husband, Gordon, was an oil rig geologist. For a while he and I swapped rig stories, and he gave me his analysis on who was to blame for the BP Oil spill that was still gushing into the Gulf of Mexico at the time of our trek. From there we turned to Climate Change, and then to the disappearing glaciers of Kilimanjaro.

"What Gore did not say about Kilimanjaro in *An Inconvenient Truth* was that the ice fields were in retreat long before human-caused Global Warming supposedly got started," Gordon said.

"But now tropical glaciers are retreating all around the world, right? This isn't just happening in East Africa." I responded.

"And on Kilimanjaro," Mike, the other Canadian, jumped in, "the rate of retreat has doubled in the last forty years. So whatever force started the glacier melt here has been accelerated by Climate Change." It turned out Mike was an avid ice climber and knew a lot about glaciers. "From the reports I've read," he continued, "in the past 11,700 years Kilimanjaro has never been free of ice. This is a change in epochs."

"I'm not saying there's no Climate Change," insisted Gordon, "just that there are too many unknowns on Kilimanjaro. For example, there are no long-term measurements of air temperature at the summit. We don't know if the air is really warming up there or not. Without the data, you can't draw conclusions. There might be other factors–increased solar radiation or decreased snowfall. It might be that Climate Change is affecting humidity over the Indian Ocean, and that's causing long-term increases in dryness in East Africa. We just don't know."

"But what if by the time there's enough evidence to convince all the skeptics, it's too late?" grumbled Mike.

We dropped the conversation as the bus climbed the hills, now pixilated with patchwork squares of field and forest. It felt exciting to be entering the wilderness at last. I looked out the window as we sped past rows upon rows of tall, straight reddish-brown trunks. Something seemed strange. Looking closer, I could see the trees were all one species, all one height.

"That's not a real forest," pronounced Marita, the German

woman. She had brown eyes and short brown hair, and seemed to be in her late twenties.

She was right. These were tree plantations, not natural forest. It was timber grown for the purpose of harvesting. Around a bend, we saw a hilltop had been freshly clear cut. Dead branches littered the roadside like broken bones.

"People are chewing up the jungle," said Bastian, Marita's companion. He had a shaved head, and looked young, muscular, and incredibly fit. He spoke English slowly, deliberately, with a thick accent that made me think of the Terminator: "Tearing it *down* and chewing it *up*."

"It's the same all across Africa," chimed in Ian, one of the silver-haired New Zealanders. He wore an earring in one ear. "But at least here they are replanting. That's something."

"Yeah," drawled Bryce the young Aussie, "But logging's supposed to be illegal on Kilimanjaro."

"Really?" I said. In the back of the bus, we were all incredulous, having already seen so many villagers carrying loads of firewood on their heads.

"A few years back the president of Tanzania declared a moratorium on all logging on Kilimanjaro," Bryce continued. "But there's a million people living in Moshi, Arusha, and these foothills. They need wood for building and fuel for cooking. Charcoal was a main industry here."

"You mean, people cut down the rainforest to make *charcoal*?" I asked, stunned.

"Yeah," Bryce nodded. "My parents used to work in Tanzania, they told me about what's been happening. Like Gordon said, there's been a fierce drought in East Africa for the past few years. But even in a drought, the rivers from Kilimanjaro used to keep flowing. This time, they are drying up too. Most of the farming around here is from irrigation, not rainfall, so their crops have failed. They have had to resort to cutting firewood in the forest and selling it just to earn a living.

This just increases deforestation. It's a lucky break the rains came back this spring. But next year, who knows?"

"I've read that the deforestation increases the drought, too," added Mike. "Until about fifty years ago, all the experts thought glacier melt was the source of Kilimanjaro's rivers. But scientists have since discovered that the glaciers provide very little water to the land below. Less than one percent of it. Most of the melting ice just evaporates in the thin air. It's the forests on the mountain-sides that make the difference."

"Of course, it rains on the rainforests," I said.

"That's not it," Mike continued. "The two short rainy seasons last only a few months of the year. But the valleys around Kilimanjaro stay green year round. See, the higher-elevation forest we are headed into is not a rainforest, it's a *cloud* forest. Cloud forests do this amazing thing called *fog stripping*. Moisture from the clouds collects as dew on the broad leaves of trees and ferns. These plants act like funnels. The water drips down to the forest floor which sucks it up like a giant, saturated sponge. Fog stripping pulls an incredible amount of moisture from the sky on Kilimanjaro, about 500 million tons of water per year. So even in the dry season, the rivers flow from the forest into the valley."

"But then, what caused the local droughts?" asked Vanessa.

"Deforestation, like Bryce said," Mike continued. "The leaves of the lower level forest give off moisture through evaporation. The winds bring that moist air up the mountainside where it turns to cloud, and the cloud forest draws it down into the soil where it trickles into the rivers, then back down to the lowlands in a perfect cycle. But when you cut down the trees you reduce the mechanism for cycling moisture through the air. Deforestation has been so extensive now that when there's a drought in East Africa, it affects Kilimanjaro like never before."

"So it is human-made climate change, at the local level," said Vanessa, shaking her head. "I can see what will happen. When the forests are gone, the winds will just blow the moisture away, onto the plains. The rains will end and the green will disappear from Kilimanjaro."

Four hours after our departure from Moshi the bus bumped through the Londorossi Gate entrance to Kilimanjaro National Park. It was crowded with several other tourist groups and perhaps a hundred porters. They milled about, hollering noisily in local dialects while uniformed park rangers weighed and tallied every bag. We climbed out of our bus and into the chaos, stretching out the kinks and griping about the long drive and the uncomfortable seats. A large truck arrived right behind us, the back of it filled with our porters, about thirty of them. Some of them sat on boxes of supplies and our gear bags. The rest had been standing through the bumpy ride, hanging on to the sides of the truck. They jumped down and started unloading the bags into the melee. Watching them, I felt a bit less inclined to whine about my stiff back.

A short, copper-skinned man wearing a baseball cap called out to us in English above the din, "Welcome to Kilimanjaro! Lunchtime!"

This was Fred, the man who was to be our guide. He and two other guides handed round white cardboard lunchboxes to the twelve tourists on our bus who eagerly gathered round. I liked Fred instinctively. The top of his head came up level with my nose, so he must have been about five foot three. He had almond-shaped eyes and dark, close-cropped hair under his cap, which he never took off. For all I knew he was bald on top. A thin black moustache hung above his broad, friendly smile that played on his lips, as if he were about to let you in on a joke.

As I took my lunchbox from Fred's hands, I asked him why the park rangers were weighing all the bags. Fried explained in near-fluent English that it is forbidden to leave trash behind on the mountain. Every bag is weighed on the way in and on the way out. And if the numbers don't tally right, the company must pay a big fine.

Josh and I took our lunches and sat with the others from our bus on three weathered old picnic tables under the shelter of a tall tree. The boxes contained a piece of greasy fried chicken, a hardboiled egg, some biscuits, a pack of peanuts, a mango-flavored juice box, a tiny banana, and a little, cold hamburger wrapped in cellophane. Josh peeled off the wrapper and tentatively bit into the burger.

"How is it?" I asked.

"It looks sad and it tastes odd," he said, chewing reflectively. "But it goes so well with the baby bananas, like it's some kind of mini African Happy Meal."

I bit into mine. It had a slightly pungent taste, a bit goaty, a bit gamey. Not spoiled, just weird, like a new flavor of beef I had never tried before.

Fred told us to each sign the big tourist registration book by the glass window of the rangers' station. I flipped through the pages. I counted the names of 53 tourists signed in the same day as us to start the trek on the two western routes to the summit. Fred told me roughly 300 tourists start the climb on six trails each day during the six-month trekking season. About 90 percent choose the shortest and easiest route, Marangu, which can be done in four to five days, while the other trails typically take six to eight days and require pitching tents along the way. Marangu features permanent huts with bunk beds and soft drinks for sale at every rest stop, which is why the porters and guides call it the 'Coca Cola Route.'

I did the math: 300 tourists a day, with about five porters, guides and cooks per tourist. Each trek lasts on average six days during climbing season. That meant on any given day during the six-month climbing season about 9,000 Tanzanians were employed by trekking companies on the mountain. Even a low estimate of $11 per day for wages and tips would be almost $100,000 each day, or $18 million a year. Factor in jobs created in hotels, growing and preparing food for 9,300 people on the mountain per week. Include the drivers, merchants, launderers, souvenir sellers, park rangers, and other administrative jobs related to the tourist trade. Adding it all up in my head, I realized Kilimanjaro not only creates its own weather, it also creates its own thriving economy. (I was not far off. I later came across a study by the Overseas Development Institute in January 2009, which estimated that 35,000 to 40,000 people visit Kilimanjaro every year, spending almost $50 million annually in Tanzania. The Tanzania Park Service calculated 46,856 tourists climbed Kilimanjaro in the 2009/10 climbing season).

On top of the local benefits, the park service charged each trekker $100/day for climbing permits, plus a $25/day rescue-insurance fee that together sent about $25 million per year to the central government. It made sense now, the logging ban, and the care with which supplies were being measured to prevent littering. The government had good reason to protect this huge generator of wealth. Instead of allowing the mountain to be treated like a dump, the government recognized its pristine beauty as the main draw for tourists. They knew not to kill the goose that lays their golden eggs–even if there were far from successful at keeping the local people from cutting down trees in the foothills. But would the tourists still come, I wondered, when the glaciers disappeared?

The park rules were posted on a giant wooden sign. Most of them were words of advice about altitude sickness, advising tourists to allow time for acclimatization, drink plenty of liquids, and descend immediately in case of severe symptoms. A second sign read simply: *POLE, POLE*, pronounced "*po*-lay, *po*-lay," with the emphasis on the first syllable. Fred, told us it was Swahili for the golden rule, the one Ezekiel had revealed to us last night: 'Slowly, slowly,' our mantra for climbing Kilimanjaro.

"I hear," said Mike, "that the single toughest thing for Tanzanian guides is preventing Western tourists from trying to race to the top as fast as they can so they don't get altitude sickness."

"I bet that can get ugly, "I said.

"Of course,' said Bastian, in his slow, Terminator voice. "People die."

It took almost two hours before the guides loaded us back in the bus. We drove another hour to the Lemosho Glades, the starting point for our trek, at an elevation of 2,100 meters. Josh and I had debated which route to the top would be best for us, and we chose Lemosho because it is the only one of the six routes that takes hikers through rainforest, allowing us to experience the whole range of Kilimanjaro's different environments.

"Wild elephant, buffalo, and giraffe live in the forest," Fred told us as we bounced along the increasingly rough track. "A few years ago, a black rhino was spotted in the hills. Even the lion or the leopard sometimes passes through. Some tour companies make their guides bring a gun. But not ours. It's not really necessary."

The only wildlife we saw that afternoon was a gang of lanky colobus monkeys hanging out in the branches of a giant camphorwood tree. We got out of the bus to take a look. They had long, shaggy hair that seemed to flow from their shoulders like capes: white, but with a broad black stripe down their backs, like reverse skunks. Their faces and tails were white. They looked weirdly elegant as they leaped about in the trees.

"They look like Goths," said Josh.

"More like flying skunks than monkeys," said Marita with a laugh.

"Let's call them Skonkies," said Josh.

We all stared at them. They stopped their graceful bouncing around on the branches and stared back at us.

"I wonder, what do they see when they look at us?" mused Bryce.

"Ohhh, look at the no-tail monkeys!" said Josh in a cartoonish voice, "Hmmm…all wound up in some kind of cotton plant and stuff made from nasty-smelling dried tar goo. No fur to keep them warm. Their poor feet seem to be wrapped in the skins of dead pigs. It's disgusting! They can't climb trees like that. And those stubby little arms and tiny little hands just hang down at their sides, no use for grabbing branches. How could they survive, not swinging in trees, not flipping from branch to branch with the greatest of ease?"

We laughed and the startled skonkies bounced on their branches, leapt into the air, and flew away into the forest.

The road was now rutted and slippery. The driver swerved around hippo-sized potholes. Before long the wheels were just spinning in muck. We got out. The driver reversed, and then drove our bus back down the hill.

"Now what?" I asked Fred.

"Now we walk," he said.

"But Fred, it's getting close to three o'clock, and we're not even at the trailhead. I'm concerned we will end up hiking in jungle in the dark."

Fred looked at me with a big, beaming smile. "*Hakuna matata!*" he said.

Behind me, Josh called out, "No problem!"

"Josh, you speak Swahili!" Fred laughed.

"Fred, the whole world knows *hakuna matata!*"

He and Bryce chimed in together on the Disney song's chorus. Josh mimed Pemba the cartoon warthog's deep gravelly voice. I must have listened to that soundtrack a thousand times back when Josh was a kid. Now here we were, in the land of *The Lion King*, where *hakuna matata* was the real-life "problem-free philosophy."

After an hour of walking, a seven-seat jeep with the name of our tour company stenciled on the side in yellow paint met us on the road. Fred and the other two guides packed all twelve of us into it. The three of them clambered onto the rear bumper and held on with their hands. We took off, skidding and lurching up the track. Josh stood up in the middle of the vehicle with five or six others, his head and shoulders stuffed out of the open sun roof. It must have looked as if the jeep were an overcrowded jack-in-the-box. I was mashed in the rear seat between Marita and Vanessa. We were unable to budge, unable to see for the bodies crammed in right in front of us. Trees and bushes whipped by, smacking the side windows. Josh and the other standing room passengers ducked and held up their arms to shield their faces. Occasionally the jeep would slither and bump hard, slamming those of us in the backseat side to side, crunching our hipbones into each other. Marita laughed as if she were riding a Tilt-a-Whirl.

"Well, we are really getting to know each other now!" she said.

Where the last of the road disintegrated, the jeep slid to a stop. We peeled ourselves apart, stretched out the kinks again. A thin, red-earth footpath trail cut into the rainforest. I checked my watch. At 4:30 p.m. we officially began our trek.

The late afternoon sun poured in between the branches of juniper and wild olive trees, creating contrasting patches of dark and light green. Unlike the plantations below, there were dozens of tree species here, some with peeling bark and tiny blooming flowers, white, yellow and red. Swathes of pale green bearded lichen draped from the tree limbs like moldering old bed sheets hung out to dry in the forest and long forgotten. At odd moments rays from the dropping sun would reflect off these sheets, lighting then up with a flash of brilliant chartreuse. At our feet, tiny, delicate orchids with purple and pink petals dotted our path. Coarse, big-leaved plants, waist high, turned out to be some kind of African nettle. Standing aside to let some porters pass, I brushed against one. I felt a prickle of electricity. Looking down, my arm was covered with miniature translucent barbs. Birdsong filled the air, and the occasional high-pitched nasal braying of a hornbill blasted overhead. On the forest floor I almost tromped on a living stream of large, brown safari ants.

At first the twelve of us chatted and chattered, still getting to know each other, telling our stories as travelers do naturally when thrown together in a temporary, baboon-like troop. Ian and Philippa told me about their hairdressing business in New Zealand, which had grown so successful that they could take off for a few months each year to indulge their lifelong passion for travel. In their hippy twenties, they had even driven by car from Cairo to Capetown. I felt this sweet, easy bond between them from having lived a life of adventure together. I could only hope Teresa and I would spend our sixties like this.

Mike talked about his love of teaching at a grade school at a small native community in the far north of Quebec. He described how he had acquired a reputation within his adopted community as a rather peculiar person because of his passion for ice climbing the local cliffs in the middle of winter. I caught a paradoxical sense of him as a loner seeking to test his limits, yet dedicated to serving others.

Aussie Bryce turned out to be a hotshot computer geek. He worked for an international IT consulting firm. He told Josh and me about a service call he recently made to Russia's space agency to help them fix a satellite. He ended up working at the same control room from which Sputnik was launched. He was just 23 years old, wiry, talking constantly. On the bus he had been restless, compulsively bouncing his leg. He seemed to have an inexhaustible supply of energy. He had burning blue eyes and a firm belief in his own indestructibility that was a bit frightening. He told us this trip up Kilimanjaro was preparation for an Everest expedition he had been invited to join in the fall as the team's computer expert. He was a vertical cliff climber, but had little experience in high altitudes. Kilimanjaro was his warm-up climb. I found myself wishing Josh had a bit of Bryce's drive to overachieve. But at the same time, I could only bear to listen to the Aussie rattle on about his adventures for ten minutes or so before I needed a break from his manic energy.

I noticed Bryce wore a brace on his right knee. I asked him why.

"Aw, just some weak tendons," he said. "Every now and then the knee pops right out of its socket. Bloody hell! All of a sudden, it just goes sideways. Always a bit of a pain to pop it back in again. So I've got to be a bit cautious, you see?"

Funny how travelling together allows people to share their stories in a way that is much more revealing than ordinary life. After a few hours, I felt I knew more about my travelling companions than I did about my neighbors in my Washington suburb–people I've lived next door to for several years. I drifted back into Bryce's conversation. He was explaining to Josh what his plans were after climbing the mountain.

"I also wanted to see this orphanage in Moshi," he said. "My parents worked in Tanzania a long time ago. Before they left, they started this orphanage. It's still running, so I wanted to take a look.

"What about you, mate? What do you do?" Bryce asked Josh.

I tuned in, curious to hear how Josh described himself to a stranger.

"Well, I've been doing acting all my life. So I'm a theater major. A lot of what I love to do is music, too. I play piano and accordion. I sort of taught myself to play. I also love writing music and a lot of what I do is my own stuff. And then as a career, sort of on the side, I do massage therapy. I really enjoy it, and people tell me I have a knack for it, so I studied it, got licensed for it. I did that because I decided if I'm going to be dedicating my life to theater and music, I should also do something that has an income and that I enjoy. So, um, that's what I do."

So, that was Josh in thirty seconds. Listening, I got the sense that his thumbnail sketch was not just a description of what he does, it was also an outline of the life ahead of him. How fortunate, at twenty, to have such a clear sense of where he is going, I thought, which talents he was going to develop and rely upon to make his way in the world. It occurred to me that this is rather rare. Most of his friends don't have such clear vision of themselves. Certainly, when I was in my late teens and early twenties, what I wanted to do with my life changed radically from year to year.

I fell in next to our guide and asked him about his life. Fred told me he had been working on Kilimanjaro for five years. He started as a porter, then waiter, cook, assistant guide and finally full guide. I liked hearing that there was room for promotion in the Tanzanian trekking biz, that on Kilimanjaro, a man like Fred could work his way to the top. His near-fluent English was obviously a big asset. Most of the local porters spoke little English, Fred said, which was surprising to me, given that Tanzania was a former British colony with English still the official language.

"So how did you learn such good English?" I asked.

"I was fortunate," Fred told me. "I didn't go to a government school. You don't learn anything there. My parents are farmers. They had no money for education. A rich foreigner sponsored me so I could go to a private Lutheran school in Tanga, by the coast."

More porters caught up with us. We stood aside on the trail to allow them to march ahead. They were tall, thin, sinewy men with dark chocolate skin–Chaggas, like Ezekiel, the native people of Kilimanjaro. They looked so much different than Fred who was shorter and with much lighter skin. The porters dressed in faded and worn mountain equipment, doubtless donated by previous climbers. It was good to see they all wore proper hiking shoes, rather than the canvas runners or sandals I had seen on the feet of porters in Nepal the previous summer, when I had trekked through the remote Kingdom of Mustang to the border of Tibet.

"*Jambo!*" each man gave us the traditional Swahili greeting as he blew past us on the trail. The porters balanced heavy sacks and gear bags on their heads, with their personal gear swinging from small rucksacks on their backs. In age they ranged–well, I suppose from Josh's age to my age.

"It's going to be hard to get to know them without much language in common," I mused.

"In their own company," Fred explained, "after a day carrying gear up the mountain, they like to laugh and joke and tease each other. It's a hard job, sure, but in the evening, a good time. But sometimes tourists want to share a meal. Then the porters feel they have to sit polite and quiet," Fred turned to look at me and pulled a glum face. "They don't speak English, and it's rude to talk before the guests in their own language. They try to smile, but you know, it's kind of extra work, after work is supposed to be finished for the day. So…"

"I get the message. Just let them do their job."

As the path steepened, conversation dropped and then resumed again on the downhill slopes. I puffed heavily and had to concentrate on finding a solid place to plant each boot. Our bodies fell into a single rhythm, like soldiers falling in step. We gradually spread out along the path. Soon Josh and I found ourselves walking alone with each other.

"You know what song I have stuck in my head?" Josh said to me as we trudged along. 'Sugar…dada dada da da…Oh, honey, honey.' "

"The Archies song? From the seventies? I didn't even know you knew it."

"Yeah, it's stuck. I can't get it out."

"Like a broken record?"

"Record? Seriously, Dad?" he laughed.

"Okay, like an iPod stuck on replay?"

We crossed over a small stream, splashing our boots.

"You know, this sense of having something stuck in your head is a good place to start talking about memes. You ready for it?"

"Sure," Josh replied. "Maybe it will take my mind off the song."

"So, what do you know about memes?"

"It's stuff from the Internet. A meme is something that gets picked up online and goes viral. Like a YouTube video sent around on Facebook. Or an emoticon, something like that."

"These are great examples, and it's more than that, too. A meme is a special kind of idea. It's an idea we can pass on to other people, things like information, skills, facts, gossip, scientific knowledge. Replicability—that's the key feature of a meme. Think of it in terms of writing a song. If you are just singing a tune you made up in your head, it's not a meme. But if you sing it to someone else, and they start humming it themselves—now you've created a meme.

"Why call it 'meme'?"

"The term was coined in 1976 by a philosopher of science named Richard Dawkins. Dawkins chose it because the word shares the same root as 'memory' and 'mimic,' but also because it kind of rhymes with 'gene.' It was his insight that ideas function like mind-genes. Genes are bits of DNA that are passed from parent to child. Memes are bits of mental DNA that are passed from one mind to another. Genes form the building blocks of biological life. Memes are the building blocks of human culture. Like genes, memes replicate and spread. Successful memes spread widely and get passed on to many minds. That's what we mean when we say something 'goes viral.' As memes compete with each other for space in our individual minds, human culture evolves."

"Like survival of the fittest?"

"Right. Like a pop song making it to the top of the charts, a new fashion catching on, a scientific theory gaining acceptance, or a political ideology gaining popular support.

"It sounds like *everything* is a meme."

No, just the ideas we pass along. These can be small, simple ideas like words, jokes, axes, or large complex ideas, like computers, math, medicine–"

"But an ax isn't an idea." objected Josh.

"True. The *physical* ax isn't a meme. From a meme point of view, the physical ax is a 'vehicle' that carries the *idea* of an ax. Think of it this way: Imagine caveman Bob is the first hominid to use a broken rock to scrape something. Others watch, they learn to chip stones themselves and pass the idea along to their tribe members. It spreads to every tribe they come in contact with – not by physical evolution, but from mind to mind. Sometime later, cavewoman Betty gets the idea to tie a sharpened rock to the end of a stick. The innovation spreads, and before you know it, everyone is using the new ax meme. The idea gets passed on, and as it does, it evolves. In fact, as far as we can tell, the chipped sharp stone is the first meme our ancestors invented–an idea that was being passed on at least 2.6 million years ago.

I was panting and sweating. Walking, talking and thinking at the same time was proving hard work. We paused on the trail. I took a swig of water and passed my bottle to Josh.

"So here's the important point," I continued. "While most other species depend on their genes to evolve, we humans evolve in two ways: through biological adaptation driven by our genes, and through cultural adaptation driven by our memes. Genetic change is slow. It spreads one generation at a time. Memetic change is fast. A new idea can spread through a whole society in a single generation. That's lightning-speed compared to genes. Think of the hundreds of thousands of years it took for elephants to evolve their big tusks. Now in a sense they are stuck with them. The human mind can evolve the technology of making sharp rocks, but then in an evolutionary blink of an eye, we can switch when a better tool comes along."

"Like from record player to ipods."

"Exactly. So, memeticists–the folks who think and write about memes–believe memes gave us amazing flexibility to adapt to our environment. This drove our physical evolution towards bigger brains which were better containers of memes. While other animals were evolving claws and fangs, we were evolving vast neural networks with hundreds of billions of nerve cells swelling our cerebral cortex, bulging out the front of our skulls. Each nerve cell in our head connects to on average one hundred others, making an estimated 100 trillion possible connections in our brains. This huge evolutionary push has made the human brain the most complex living thing alive, infinitely more complex than the most powerful computer."

"100 trillion, huh?" Josh sounded skeptical.

"Literally, the number of possible nerve cell connections in each human head is greater than the total number of particles in the universe."

The light was starting to fade. I had forgotten how quickly night falls in the tropics, how different from the long hours of summer sunlight back home. Some of our companions had thought to bring their headlamps with them, but Josh and I had packed our lamps in our duffle bags, which were with the porters. This was the perfect way to twist an ankle on some invisible tree root in the dark. It was exactly the sort of situation I had been afraid we would be facing due to our late start on the trail.

Fred came up behind us.

"How much further?" I asked him with an edge of irritation in my voice. "We can't see anymore."

"*Hakuna matata*, my friend!" Fred said.

Josh laughed. "Dad, *that's* a meme gone global!"

Fred pulled his own headlamp out of his pack, and shone it like a spotlight on our feet as we trudged along in the darkening gloom. We had to stop talking, focusing all our attention just on our feet.

We heard the camp before we saw it: a human humming that filled the forest, a weird, overlapping, rippling mix of English,

German, Dutch, Swahili and many other languages all jumbled together. At a clearing we could see glowing light from some thirty tents. They were packed so closely together amongst the tall trees you could not walk between them for fear of getting tangled in the peg lines. This was Camp Mti Mkubwa, which means "Big Tree." We split up from our companions as each separate group followed their guides into the camp and disappeared in the darkness.

"This way," Fred indicated with a swing of his headlamp beam, guiding us towards our small, blue, two-man tent.

Our duffle bags were laid out on the plastic floor liner at the front opening. We crept inside and pulled our bags in after us. We rummaged around for our lamps and fleece jackets. The temperature had dropped quickly in the dark, now that we were at 2,700 meters above sea level. We shivered and quickly pulled on our warm outer clothing.

A Chagga man in a fuzzy leopard-print hat brought us two plastic bowls of heated water and indicated by mime that we were to use it to wash our sweaty faces and dirty hands. When we were clean, Fred appeared and told us to follow him. By flashlight he took us over to a small green tent the size of a phone booth. Unzipping it with a flourish, Fred shone the light on a white plastic portable toilet with a hand pump flush on the side. It was for our personal use, he explained. This meant we would not have to use the primitive, smelly, squat-over-the-hole style sheds that served as outhouses for most tourists at the mountain campsites.

I was aghast. Never in my life have I had a designated, personal porta-potty, let alone a designated potty-porter to carry my private loo up a mountain top. I had no idea this was included in the tour package. Had I been given the choice I would never have asked for it. I felt a peculiar stab of discomfort. It was the twinge I get when something is happening that appears out of synch with my idea of who I am: the do-it-yourself Canadian who sees all people as equal. I had an impulse to tell Fred to send the toilet back down the trail. And what, put a man out of work for a week?

"I don't know about this, Josh," I said, shaking my head. "I traveled alone in Europe and Asia for so many years. I felt so self-reliant. Now I've got somebody carrying my toilet. It's not going to be easy to get used to. It seems so, I don't know, colonial, like some English gentlemen on safari 100 years ago. Where are the crystal goblets and the silver candelabras?"

"What? No candelabras? Jeez, Dad, you should have warned me. I tell you what, you totally have my permission to poop in the woods if it makes you feel good. Now, excuse me a moment, cause I have to pee in the tent."

A half hour later, Fred summoned us to a much larger green tent and opened the zipper for us with a flourish. Inside we found two blue folding camp chairs set on either side of a small wooden table. It was covered with a blue cotton tablecloth loaded with tea, coffee, Milo (the British powdered cocoa drink), powdered milk, ketchup, mustard and a steel thermos full of hot water. A single burning candle had been affixed to the top of a tin of mushrooms, providing the only light. Fred left us alone inside.

"A Kilimanjaro candelabra!" observed Josh.

A plate of fresh-popped popcorn with crumbly chocolate biscuits on top had been placed in the center.

"Is this dinner?" asked Josh.

"I dunno," I said. "Probably it's our *amuse bouche.*"

We munched. The popcorn was still warm. It tasted light and fresh, with none of the heavy butter-and-salt flavor that drenches US Cineplex popcorn or comes out of a microwavable bag. The Chagga man who had brought us our washing water entered the tent together with Fred. The Chagga was tall, with high cheek-bones, a broad nose, cheerful black eyes illuminated by the candle flame, and a beaming, friendly smile. Fred introduced him as Sully, short for Solomon, I assumed, to fit with the other

Biblical heroes who worked for our trekking company. Sully was to be our waiter for the trip, Fred said. We exchanged *Jambo!* greetings. Fred said dinner would be ready soon, and then left the tent. Sully came over to the table, pointed to our teacups, and then put his hand on the steel hot water container. He looked at us intently.

"Focus!" he said, and gave a little nod, to see if we understood. We gazed back in utter confusion. Sully flashed another smile then backed out through the flaps.

"Boy, I guess we need to get our act together," said Josh, cracking up.

"Yeah, no time for talking while there's food on the table and drinks to be poured. Oh wait, I think when he said 'focus' he meant 'thermos!' "

Sully came back a few minutes later and set before each of us a napkin, spoon, knife and fork. He did this in a peculiarly awkward way, as if unfamiliar with where to put the various items. His fingers handled the cutlery clumsily. He hesitated before making each move, his brow furrowed. Finally he decided to lay the napkin in the center of each place setting, then laid the three utensils in a row facing us, and then folded the top of the napkin down over the top parts of the silverware, covering the eating bits. Watching him work was riveting. It was as if he had never in his life laid a table with such implements before, and was improvising as he went along. When finished, he gave the table a small nod of approval, looked up at us and grinned sheepishly. Then he gracefully backed out of the tent and into the night.

"He doesn't know the memes!" said Josh. "He knows there's a pattern to this, a way foreigners expect things to be arranged, but he doesn't know what it is."

"I guess you're right. But hey, maybe Sully will hit on a new meme that will revolutionize table setting and spread round the world!"

Sully was back again in a minute with plates and two covered steel pots.

"Welcome dinner!" he announced.

He whipped off the lids to reveal spaghetti noodles in one pot, carrot stew with chunks of beef in the other. This, like so many of our later meals, seemed to be an attempt at Western-style cooking, but with a peculiar twist: carrots instead of tomatoes. But in the cold and dark of the jungle, it tasted hot and savory, and we slurped it all down.

Sully whisked back inside carrying a bowl of sliced mango and avocado.

"Welcome dessert!" he announced.

He smiled and pointed to Josh's dinner plate.

"You like pancake?"

"Suuure…I guess so." Confusion covered Josh's face.

"I think he meant 'spaghetti,' " I said as Sully left the tent.

Dinner finished, we walked to the forest edge and brushed our teeth, spitting into the jungle. Slowly we picked our way through the close-packed tents back to our own. Josh stood in front of the tent flaps, shining his headlamp across the maze of peg lines in the general direction of our portable privy. He rubbed his cheek.

"I might be able to find it, but I don't know how I would ever make it back."

"Just pee on a tree," I said wearily.

He headed back towards the edge of the clearing while I got settled inside my sleeping bag.

A few minutes later Josh threw himself inside the tent, scared and laughing hysterically.

"I saw something in the bush," he said, kicking off his boots and burrowing into his bag. "It looked big. It looked like…" he paused, recalling some nightmarish horror fixed in his mind's eye, "…like part turkey, part monkey. It was white, and all *poofy* around the edges."

"Poofy?" I laughed.

"Yes, *poofy*. But in a very scary, menacing kind of way."

"You make it sound truly terrifying. Perhaps it was a skonkie?"

"No, it was bigger than that, about three feet high and walking on all fours. It heard me and looked right at me. I shined my light on it, and saw its eyes glowing red. It was staring right back at me. I said, 'Okeeeeeee,' and slowly walked away. Now I'm afraid I'm going to dream about it."

He made a gobbling monkey sound.

"We'll have to ask Fred in the morning. Maybe he can identify it."

Soon Josh was snoring. I lay awake and thought about the many times we had shared at tent in Canada when he was a kid. It was so important to me that he had contact with the wild and wild creatures while growing up. I recalled one of my strongest memories of him during a long walk on a river trip on the Upper Stikine in Northern British Columbia. He was about nine and had been sitting alone by a stream while a group of us hiked the ridge overhead. Looking down, I saw a small herd of caribou walking up the stream. They didn't notice Josh, and soon they were grazing all around while he sat still, right in the middle of them. Watching at a distance, I felt this upwelling of joy, just witnessing his experience of connection with the wild.

My father took me into the wild when I was a child, but in a different way. He liked to hunt and fish. Whenever ducks would fly by us, he would raise an imaginary shotgun in the air and fire at them, "Bang-bang!"

One year when I was eight or nine he took me hunting with him. I remember riding in an aluminum boat at dawn through grey water and cold wind, then sitting in the bulrushes for hours. He shot some ducks and they fell from the sky. It was wonderful to me that he could do that. We motored out and he picked the birds up out of the water, throwing them in the bottom of the boat. I remember gazing at a dead male mallard, the feathers on its head and neck shimmering green, so beautiful. It made me feel a funny kind of sad in my stomach. Suddenly the head moved. I saw a wing struggling to flap.

"Dad, Dad! This one's alive!' I said. I thought maybe we could somehow save it.

My father, one hand on the motor, looked down at the duck. With a swift gesture he picked it up by its orange webbed feet, and swung it hard in an arc against the gunwale. The head cracked with a sharp thud, and he threw the carcass back in the bottom of the boat, as casually as if flicking a cigarette ash. Then he turned his attention back to our course. He did this all without speaking. I stared, transfixed at the blood oozing out from around one open, glassy eye. The boat is speeding, the motor roaring. It's cold and I'm shivering. I look at the duck, then I look at my dad, but I can't say a word.

Forty three years later, my father still keeps his wooden decoys in the basement. He tells me, though, that day he took me out with him was the last time he ever hunted ducks.

Chapter Three

On Sky Island

Day Two: Big Tree to Shira 2 Camp (3,810 meters) 18 kilometers

"Welcome hot water!"

Sully woke us at 6:30 a.m. with a washing bowl for each of us, followed by a cup of black tea which we sipped in our tent before breakfast. We had a long walk ahead of us to our second camp, 18 kilometers away. It would take us from the cloud forest up around the side of Mount Shira, Kilimanjaro's third highest cone, and from there across a vast lava plateau to our destination.

I pulled back the tent flaps and stood up. Outside, the fog was so thick I could not see across the campsite. The surrounding tents just faded into milky grey. On the periphery they disappeared. But the noise of breakfast chatter and clattering cutlery filled the soupy air. I picked my way through obstacle course of peg lines in the general direction of our little toilet tent. It was a surprisingly clean and pleasant experience. As I exited the flaps I noticed one of our porters sitting outside holding a toilet brush in a rubber-gloved hand. (I would later learn that the young man's name was Nathaniel). He got up as soon as he saw me leave, paused for a beat, and then headed towards the toilet tent. I gave a half-hearted little wave in his direction. It didn't occur to me that the toilet porter would also double as men's room attendant, nor that he would be on stake-out each morning while I visited the tent. I felt that twinge again. I made a mental note to scour the toilet bowl myself each morning, and that I would double the tip for Nathaniel at the end of our trip.

"Welcome breakfast!" Sully beamed upon my return.

He ushered us into the dining tent, and fussed with the silverware again.

Breakfast started with millet porridge. It was dark reddish-brown, thick as mud, with a hearty whole grain taste that was nutty and slightly sweet. Next to the pot was a plate of cold pancakes rolled up like crepes. No syrup, so we ate the pancakes plain with our fingers. Sully served us fried eggs with two small, crimson colored wieners on the side. Their fiery-red coats indicated some kind of unnatural, potentially radioactive substance. I tried a bite. The meat felt spongy in my mouth. It tasted like baloney that had been left in the sun too long. Already suspicious of what they put inside of hot dogs in the US, I could not imagine what animals' bits of hoof and bone must be ground up in the Tanzanian version. Josh gobbled his down and then eyed mine. I forked them over and he finished them all.

"Friend, you like? *Bwana*! Good!" Sully beamed at Josh's empty plate and gave the thumbs up sign.

"*Bwana* wiener, Sully," said Josh, returning the gesture.

"Good morning friends!" announced Fred, entering through the tent flaps like an impresario bursting through the curtains and onto the stage. "It is time! Let us go and get an early start. Today we have a lot of walking!"

Our plan was to break off from the other groups we had hiked in with and follow our own separate schedule. We wanted to say goodbye to our friends before we left, so Fred talked to the other guides and soon found the breakfast tent of our companions in the midst of the maze. Eight of them were packed tightly together around a table. They cheered when they saw us. They were on a slightly slower route to the top, taking an extra day to acclimatize before the summit. That allowed them a later start this morning, although Fred said our paths would intersect again after the summit. The Germans, Martia and Bastian, were on a faster schedule than ours and they had left camp ahead of us.

"Before we go," said Josh, "I have to tell you a scary story."

His eyes widened and they all hushed as he told of his encounter with the turkey-monkey.

 "Might it have been a baby rhino?" suggested Vanessa, when the laugher died down.

"Or a leopard," said Bryce. "Perhaps one of the legendary poofy leopards of Kilimanjaro?"

We waved goodbye, wishing each other success and safety on the way to the top.

Mike followed us out of the tent.

"Here," he said to me, thrusting several sheets of smudged and wrinkled paper into my hand. "It's that recent *Nature Magazine* article on Kilimanjaro's glaciers I was talking about with you and Gordon yesterday on the bus. I'm finished with it. You seemed interested, so I wanted to pass it on."

I thanked him and we shook hands.

Our tent was already being broken down by the porters as we hoisted our day packs on our backs and set off with Fred into the jungle. The mist still hung thick in the cool air as we started to climb the steep hillside. We could barely see ten paces ahead. Trees and branches loomed out of the fog and receded behind us. It was strange to feel this sense of claustrophobia on a mountain.

Josh told Fred about the turkey-monkey. He listened carefully as Josh described the strange creature.

"Probably a bush pig," he mused." They have bristles all over, and they have white hairs on their faces. The boars get that big, to about 50 kilos (110 pounds)."

"I guess the poofiness could have been pig bristles," said Josh, sounding skeptical and a little deflated that his encounter in the forest had been with nothing more ferocious than a wild pig.

"Are they dangerous?" I asked.

"Not really. There was one French tourist–this was very funny–in the middle of the night, a bush pig came into her tent looking for food. She ran out of the tent, just screaming!"

Fred chuckled fondly at the memory.

The path rose and fell over a series of streams and forested valleys. Large trees draped with beards of moss covered over the path so that at times we seemed to be walking through a green tunnel. The air remained chilly as the mist gradually cleared, which made walking easy as we climbed uphill. Fred pointed out orange gladiolas, begonia vines with white and pink flowers, and an Impatiens Kilimanjari, which he said was locally known as the "elephant flower." We stooped to examine the bright red tip of it. The flower appeared to have two large, red floppy ears, with a long yellow trunk coming down from the bottom, curling at the end, just like an elephant's nose.

"This elephant flower is found nowhere else in the world, only on Kilimanjaro," Fred said with a tinge of pride in his voice.

"Why only here?" asked Josh.

"Kilimanjaro is a sky island," Fred replied. Like an island far away in the ocean, like Australia, you will find special plants that grow only here, because of the altitude, and nowhere else."

The path steepened and we adjusted our pace to a steady, vigorous climb. We stripped down to t-shirts and soon fell into a rhythm that worked our legs and our lungs. It had been a year since my last trek in the Himalayas, and my 52-year-old body was feeling the strain. Even though our day packs were light, I could feel the weight of it in my shoulders and back. I adjusted the straps compulsively. We had barely started the day's walk, and already I was thinking about how long it would take to reach our camp for the night.

"You know," Josh said, "I'm finding this walk a great time to put into practice something I learned in my body movement class this year called The Alexander Technique."

"Tell me about it."

"It's basically retraining your body to move like it did when you were a little kid. As adults, we get locked into habits of movement from work and school, like sitting for hours and hours at a computer, doing mindless repetitive stuff. We get so focused on completing a task that we cut ourselves off from our bodies. We don't even notice when we are locked into a position. We slouch, or curve our back in a way we weren't meant to, just pushing to get the job done. The Alexander Technique teaches your body to become less goal-oriented. For instance, you walk with your whole body. It's not just the leg's job to carry you to your destination. You can tense up your whole leg, stomp your foot down, pull your body up with your whole lower back. But that's like using a flamethrower to light a candle. When you bring awareness into how much effort you're expending with each movement, you realize you don't need to use so much. You can just lift your leg. You can let your foot reach the ground at its own pace without slapping it there as quick as possible. You can let that movement carry up through the rest of your body and just move you up and forward."

"I'll give it a try."

The trail wound up and down the undulating hills, taking us higher and higher. I noticed that while climbing I could lean forward a little and let gravity push me forward. I'd just move my leg up to catch me and push me up a little bit. It was kind of like gliding up the hill, almost like riding an escalator. As we ascended the forest canopy opened up, with fewer and fewer big trees. These gradually gave way to thickets of cypress-like evergreen bushes. They had twisted narrow trunks with tufts of dull green leaves, like giant gnarly green candy floss cones constructed for some animated Tim-Burton-nightmare movie. We felt direct sunlight on our shoulders for the first time.

At the crest of a flat hilltop we broke into sunlight and blue sky. We looked back and saw a layer of mist below us. It was not that the fog had cleared. Instead we had climbed above it. Cloud covered the lower slopes and stretched back across the entire valley floor. It struck me as funny to think that just yesterday we were looking up at these clouds. Fred declared a short break. We wandered around looking for some rocks to sit on to drink our little boxes of mango juice and munch a few biscuits. We came across a dark-haired European tourist sitting in the dirt with a laptop. His guide crouched next to him, pointing a portable antenna at the sky.

"You're online?" I asked, incredulous.

"You bet," he grinned at me. "I get even the best satellite reception in Africa on the mountains."

Nearby, sheets of iridescent solar cells were scattered on the ground like hi-tech laundry squares lying out in the sun to dry. Each sheet was plugged in to cell phones, a battery pack, or some other electronic device. He turned his attention away from us and resumed tapping vigorously at the keyboard.

Josh and I found a few smooth rocks to sit on. We opened our pack of biscuits.

"This guy really makes me laugh," I said. "Can't he just leave it behind for a week? One of the reasons I like to trek is exactly to get away from email and Facebook and the sense of being constantly plugged in. I need to unplug, and it's frankly impossible for me to do it when there's a connection available. I worry that pretty soon one will be able to get online anywhere in the world. Then where do I go to escape the memes?"

"Escape? I thought you were all about the memes?"

"No, I think memes are a double-edged sword. Yesterday you couldn't get *Sugar Sugar* out of your head. You see, memes are tenacious. The memes we have today are the product of competitive evolution that's gone on in our brains for over two million years, back to stone axes, remember? While some memes are beneficial, or just plain amusing, a lot of others get into our heads and we can't get rid of them. Some writers even describe them as akin to viruses that infect the mind. Humans have gotten pretty good and engineering memes to be mental space invaders."

"Like advertising?"

"Yes, exactly. Advertising is all about infecting consumers

with memes to make them buy their products. Advertisers try to manipulate the kinds of memes they know are effective: a jingle, the image of sexy woman, a celebrity spokesperson or a doctor in a white coat saying 'take this drug and the bad feelings will go away.' There's now a whole field of advertising called Neuromarketing. Brain scientists working for advertising companies do things like wiring portable brain scanners onto subjects' heads and then sending them into shopping malls to see what parts of the brain light up when they perceive certain ads and store displays."

"That reminds me," said Josh, "of the rants that came out last year on the Internet over the new Pepsi Logo. This big-deal secret Pepsi document got released on the Web. It was the ad company's research on how to make the new logo attractive to different target audiences. It showed stuff like how the new logo incorporated everything from a smiley face to the principle of the Golden Mean. What amazed and I guess scared some people was all the work this company put into designing the logo in order to have a very specific subconscious impact on people's minds."

"Right. So what we can learn from this is that civilization is not a neutral space. It's filled with memes engineered by professionals to get into our heads and influence our behavior. When you know about memes, you have a better chance of resisting the influence of the ones you don't want. Otherwise we are swept along unconsciously under their influence. There's an amazing science fiction movie, *They Live*, which is a great metaphor for this. It's the story of an ordinary guy who finds a pair of special sunglasses. When he puts them on he sees that about 10 percent of the population is actually hideous aliens who have infiltrated the planet. He also sees that all the TV screens and billboards are really sending out messages like 'Stay Asleep,' and 'Submit to Authority.' Normal people are being hypnotized into a zombie-like trance by these alien messages. The hero has to resist the messages, fight the aliens, and break their spell over people. So like this hero, we can put on meme-aware lenses and protect ourselves from the ones we don't want to infect us."

We chewed on the last of our biscuits in silence for a minute. I was curious about Josh's response to this, but just wanted to give it time to sink in. Maybe he thought this is just Dad and another of his weird ideas. Or maybe he wasn't thinking about what I said at all. Fred told us it was time to move on.

When we resumed our walk, Fred tried to teach us a Swahili song about Kilimanjaro. (It turned out that this was a generic tourist-greeting song used all across the region. You can plug in any destination you want in Tanzania or Kenya in place of 'Kilimanjaro').

Jambo, Jambo bwana
Habari gani?
Mzuri sana
Wageni wakaribishwa
Kilimanjaro, Hakuna matata

Fred translated:

Hello, Hello Sir
How are you?
Very fine
Visitors are welcome
On Kilimanjaro, no problems!

Learning even such a simple song in another language is a great test of memes. How do you remember words in a language you don't know? It's hard. You need constant repetition. Fred laughed at how easily we forgot everything except the first and final lines. For a while we lapsed back into silence until we crested the next hill in the undulating landscape.

"Okay," Josh asked as we walked, "so how do we protect

ourselves from the memes we don't want, those mental space invaders?"

"Well, just recognizing them as memes is a big step," I said enthusiastically. "When we think that our thoughts are our own, rather than memes cycling through our brains, that's when they have a grip on us. We think that we have our thoughts. But in fact, our thoughts have us. Now, memeticists are divided as to whether we have any power to control our thoughts. Some of them think that since every concept and word is a meme, all that we are is a big meme machine. But I side with others who view the mind as more than our memes. I get this perspective from the years I spent in Buddhist and Taoist company in India, Thailand, Tibet and China, where they work with meditative states beyond the conscious mind that have nothing to do with memes. In fact, for me meme theory and eastern philosophy fit together really smoothly.

"The Taoists see the 'Tao' as an ultimate reality that's beyond words. They say 'The Tao that can be named is not the true Tao.' Yet it is possible to align yourself in harmony with the Tao. Buddhism sees all form as illusion. But it is possible to penetrate the illusion with the enlightened 'Buddha mind" that we all possess. According to both these philosophies, when we identify ourselves with our mental chatter–which the Buddhists call the 'monkey mind' but means the same as memes–we literally become lost to ourselves. To discover what our mind is like underneath all this chatter, we have to learn how to quiet the mind.

"To do this, Buddhist masters developed two basic methods of meditation. In *absorption meditation*, you focus all your awareness on a single sensation–your breath, a candle flame, a mantra (which can be any sound repeated over and over again). The idea is to ground your awareness by connecting it to a physical, constant sense impression that exists *underneath* the level of your thoughts–that is, your memes. This quiets the mind. The second method is *awareness meditation*. In awareness meditation, you observe the mental chatter as if you are standing on a bridge over top of your stream of consciousness. You just observe the thoughts flow by without getting swept along in them. When you cease to identify with the chatter, you begin to experience pure awareness, and this, too, quiets the mind.

"Taoist masters also use meditation, but it's more focused on aligning yourself with the natural energies of the Tao. So while Buddhists typically sit still to meditate, Taoists do moving meditation like Tai Chi or Qigong. This focuses their awareness directly on the subtle energy currents of the Tao. It's something I've been practicing since I lived in China 25 years ago. Retreating to nature is really important for Taoists as a way to live not exactly a meme-free existence, but a life that's not driven by them."

Josh and I were hiking well now. We had found a good pace that allowed us to walk steadily but without over-exerting ourselves and sweating. We took another break, sucking hard on our water bottles.

"How far up Kilimanjaro are we now?" Josh asked.

"Oh, this is Mount Shira, said Fred.

"We're on the wrong mountain?"

"No," Fred giggled. "Shira is the smallest of three volcanoes that make up Kilimanjaro. Shira, Mawenzi, Kibo," he counted them off on his fingers. "Kibo is the highest peak. That's the one you tourists picture when you think of Kilimanjaro. It's the biggest. It is also the only part of the volcano that is not extinct."

"What do you mean, 'not extinct'?" said Josh nervously. "Is Kilimanjaro still active?"

Fred smiled. "Kibo is not dead, just sleeping for the past 100,000 years."

"So are we climbing Shira to the top?" Josh asked.

"No, most people don't want to bother. They want to get to Kibo. So we will climb round the north slope of Shira till we reach the lava plateau. This is the western approach to Kibo. It's the long way round, but better, because the walk helps you get used to the altitude. You'll see the peak for the first time in a few more hours."

We had climbed about half way up Mount Shira's side at this point. Curving round a bend in the trail we saw Marita and Bastian, the young German couple, just ahead of us. Soon we caught up to them. On a mountain this big and this empty, finding people we already knew, even if only for a day, felt like a family reunion. We fell in together and started talking. The Germans were both in their late twenties. Bastian was an elementary school physical education teacher. Marita was a physical therapist. Bastian, the quieter of the two, was not really as much of a Terminator as I had thought. He was lean and sinewy, rather than brawny. With his smooth-shaved head, I imagined his students must think him the coolest of teachers. Though he spoke English haltingly, I sensed Bastian was also reserved, maybe even a little bit shy. Marita was more outgoing. She was vivacious, with a wide friendly smile and ready laugh. Athletically slender and fit, she had short brown hair poking out from under a green army cap. She was fluent in English, and as I already knew, she had a great sense of fun. I remembered her raucous laughter from the previous day, when we were smashed up against each other in the back seat of our careening jeep.

As we strolled along they told us about some of their adventures traveling together. They had hiked through Patagonia, along Canada's West Coast Trail, and climbed the Alps. After Kilimanjaro they were headed to the Rift Valley for a wildlife safari, then to Zanzibar and the East Africa Coast.

"So how long have you two been married?" I asked Marita.

"Oh, we aren't married. Not yet. But, after seven years together, Bastian very recently proposed. So we are getting married next month. August 27," she said brightly.

"So," I asked Bastian, "After seven years, why did you

propose now?"

Marita snorted a laugh, perhaps because I had asked the question so abruptly.

"It is common practice in Germany," Bastian shrugged. "You are together seven years. After that, if no problems, you get married, and probably it will work."

"Bastian, I think that is the most Germanic rationale for getting married I have ever heard," I said.

Marita guffawed.

"I'm so happy for you though. Travel is such a great bond to share. I'm a fortunate man that I've got this with Teresa my wife–not Josh's mom–Teresa is my second wife."

"You've traveled a lot together?" Marita asked.

"Yes. We found this great line of work that allows us to travel on the job, then when we finish, now that our kids are in college, we are free to explore."

"Well, yeah," chimed in Josh, "just as long as there are no tents or wilderness involved! Hahaha."

"Okay, fair enough!" I replied. "It's true Teresa says she appreciates wilderness best through the windows of a five-star hotel. But there's plenty to explore that excites us both."

"And you've got me for the mountains," said Josh.

We crested the side of the hill. Suddenly Kilimanjaro appeared in front of us: our first glimpse of the ice-streaked volcano since we started the trek. Even though still some 25 kilometers away, it towered over the horizon, a charcoal-grey stack of rock six kilometers (almost four miles) high. It stopped us in our tracks. For a minute we gaped in silence at what lay ahead.

A vast plateau stretched between us and the volcano, a flat grey sea of lava that had hardened some 360,000 years ago in the final, dramatic stages of Kilimanjaro's formation. About a million years ago the vast plains of East Africa were ripped apart as two of the earth's tectonic plates crashed into each other in slow motion until one buckled under and the other kicked up. The earth heaved and collapsed, forming the Great Rift Valley that runs from the Red Sea in Arabia to the Kalahari in Southern Africa–a scar across continents that is visible from space. Hot lava burst through fractures in the earth's broken crust, creating volcanic cones and craters up and down the rift, including the three that created Kilimanjaro and left behind this harsh, forbidding land.

"The trail to Mordor…On Mount Doom," said Josh in a low, ominous voice, invoking the infamous volcano from The *Lord of the Rings*. He pulled out his camera and flipped the setting to video.

"Well," he narrated brightly, panning to the distant summit, "That's where we are headed. Should take us, what, three or four hours?"

Marita faced the volcano. She stretched her arms over her head, bending her wrists inwards so that when Bastian took her picture, it looked as if she held the summit in her hands. We all laughed, and then each took our turns with the stunt. When finished, we fell silent again and just stared.

"Are we really going to climb that?" I said, quietly. "From here it does seem like its name, *Impossible to Climb*."

"Two to three hundred people do it every day," said Bastian, shrugging in a matter-of-fact way, perhaps with a fleck of distain, though the tone I picked up may merely have been his German accent.

But we all knew only about half of those who attempted actually made it to the peak.

"Do climbers really die of altitude sickness on Kilimanjaro?" Josh asked.

"Yes, sure, a few die every year," said Bastian.

"Just a few? Oh, *hakuna matata* then," Josh said with an unconvincing laugh.

The wind gusted for a moment across the lava plateau and we

felt the first ice of the glaciers. We shivered a bit.

The terrain ahead was a high-altitude moorland speckled with boulders and gorse-like, prickly brown bushes. Grey-green grasses grew in tussocks. Occasional clusters of alpine wildflowers flecked the landscape with bright daubs of yellow and white. "Everlastings," Fred called these flowers, which grew in stiff, fat clumps. They looked like frozen wedding bouquets popping up from beneath the edges of grey lumps of lava, where dust and the occasional bit of rain gave them root. Fred said these flowers grew right up to the dead zone at the edge of the volcano itself.

One tall, weird plant sprung up here and there across the surreal plateau. These were giant lobelias, which grew higher than a human and looked like pine cones on growth hormones. They had prickly, spear-like leaves on the bottom, and then bizarrely geometrical cone-shaped tops composed of spiraling leaf rosettes. Fred told us to look inside, between the leaves, at the delicate blue flowers. He said at night the leaves close up and the plant folds in on itself to protect the delicate core from the cold. The outer leaves secrete a slimy kind of moisture that freezes at night and forms a thin ice shell, keeping the interior above the frost point and enabling the plant to survive.

Our trail ran flat across the moor. It wound back and forth between boulders and twisted formations of lava that had been thrown in great molten chunks from the volcano eons ago. In places the ground grew damp and boggy, fed by springs and streams from the glaciers. We could feel the thinness of the air in our lungs now that we had climbed above 3,500 meters. At this altitude there is 40 percent less oxygen in the air than at sea level, so your lungs have to work twice as hard. When I bent down to retie a boot and then stood up, I found myself gasping for breath. The sun glared down, harsh in the thin air. With fewer air molecules, more of the sun's deadly ultraviolet rays penetrate the sky, burning your skin much more quickly than at lower altitudes. The rays will damage your eyes if you don't keep them covered with polarized lenses. The hot sun combined with the low moisture content in the high air also dries you out, leading quickly to dehydration that can amplify the effects of altitude sickness.

After about three hours of steady hiking on the plateau we arrived at a small rocky spring. Porters were bucketing out the dark water in order to boil it for tea. Lunch was being prepared. They had set folding chairs out for us in the sunshine. We stripped off our sweat-soaked socks and mopped some of the dust from our faces. Already I was feeling the burn of the sun, the dryness in my throat, and the strain from breathing so hard for so long. I sucked in the thin air, trying to regain my equilibrium. Josh lay down in the thin grass and powdery dirt, and promptly fell asleep. After a while, I nudged him with my foot.

"Hey, don't go unconscious. We still have a long way to walk."

"I'm *not* sleeping, just resting," he said without opening his eyes, but with an irritated edge in his voice.

"Well, you should cover your face with your hat. You don't want to lie exposed to the sun."

He sat up, as if grudging the interruption, then put a hand to his head.

"What is it?"

"Ah, just a bit of a headache."

"You'll feel better after we eat."

Our dining tent had been set up to keep us out of the wind, which whipped the canvas back and forth as we ate. I was glad to get into the shade. Sully appeared, welcoming lunch with his usual enthusiasm. He placed before us cold fried chicken, some doughy meat pastry, an orange and a banana, and one of the most bizarre food items we encountered on the whole trip. On each of our plates was a tennis-ball-sized oval of fried mashed potato with a deep-fried crust. The potato ball had been cut in half and set side by side on each plate to reveal a surprise inside: a hardboiled egg. It was sliced through the middle, so that the half-yolks in the center gazed out at us like a pair of giant yellow eyes. Sully beamed as we gazed with astonishment at the concoction. When he left the tent, Josh immediately reached for his camera and flipped it on video.

"You see that potato?" he narrated as he zoomed in, "There's an egg in that potato. Fuck, that's beautiful! This meme needs to reach America."

We each took a bite. The crust was greasy and hot. The potato was chewy and lukewarm. The egg was rubbery and cold. It tasted bland but we were both so hungry we devoured it all, washing down the starchy aftertaste with a box of mango juice.

We blinked as we left the tent. The sunlight had grown more intense in the afternoon, but the wind from the mountain blew cool. The lava field stretched endlessly ahead. Kilimanjaro in the distance seemed no closer than it had in the morning. Our leg muscles ached and the greasy egg-and-potatoes now sat in our bellies in a big, solid lump. We looked around for Marita and Bastian. Fred told us they had finished lunch before us, and were already well on their way to the evening camp site.

"Maybe we can catch up to them," I said.

"*Pole pole!*" Fred replied as he led off down the trail at a slow pace.

We trudged in silence for a while through the endless, other-worldly landscape littered with black chunks of lava. I imagined what it must have been like, this molten rock thrown up from the volcano millions of years ago, breaking into ten thousand pieces, spinning and freezing in midair, forming into these bizarre shapes, then crash landing upon this lava bed. I tapped the side of a formation with my knuckles as I walked past. It felt hard as steel, and hot in the afternoon sun. Long before *homo sapiens* evolved on the Kenyan plains just to the north, these rocks and this plateau existed, unchanged and unshaped through thousands of centuries. It made me feel comfortable to think about how little change humans have brought to the mountain. Until 150 years ago, when the memes of mountain climbing and then tourism developed, we had no use at all for this island in the sky.

I wanted to delve back into the realm of memes with Josh again. For an instant I thought of Teresa's skepticism about my whole meme-on-the-mountain project. But it was exactly for moments like this I was glad to have something to talk about in the hours and hours Josh and I had to cross the plateau and circle round Kilimanjaro. I was aware though that I was tending to do most of the talking, and I really wanted to hear more from him how these ideas landed and settled in his mental landscape.

"There are some memes, Josh, that have evolved into an especially resilient class," I began. "Fused into our minds as hard as this lava is fused into the ground."

"What?"

"I'm talking about our beliefs. When we believe something, we don't just hold it in our brain like a cipher, like a bit of a song or a piece of information. We fit it in with our other beliefs like a piece in a puzzle. Once a meme clicks into our minds inside a belief system, it's incredibly hard to dislodge. When a meme becomes a belief, it gains three advantages: Beliefs are tenacious. We cling to our beliefs. Beliefs repel rivals. We tend to reject other ideas that challenge our beliefs. Beliefs spread effectively. We often try to convince others to adopt our beliefs. Think for example of Galileo's discovery that the earth revolves around the sun. The Catholic Church didn't say, 'Let's study these findings.' Instead they arrested him, took him down to the dungeon and showed him the implements of torture they were going to use on him. He was seventy. He recanted. That's the power of belief. You see, for the Church this was not a matter of astronomy. Galileo's observation challenged the vertical orientation of their cosmos: hell, earth, heaven. Remove the earth from the center of creation, and you also displace God from the sky, and the devil from hell.

Replace one puzzle piece, and the whole moral cosmos of the Church falls apart–a slow process that's taken more than four hundred years so far. We see a similar conflict today with Fundamentalist Christians who reject the theory of evolution. I know, because when I was your age I was a Fundamentalist. I know what it is like to reject a scientific theory because you believe it contradicts the Word of God. If you can think of survival from a meme's point of view, becoming a belief is a great strategy."

"Dad, you really didn't believe in evolution?"

"Yep. When I was eighteen I believed Noah loaded pairs of dinosaurs on the ark! Disbelieving evolution, because I believed the Bible said otherwise, was for me a radical way of displaying my faith in God. The Creationist meme didn't stick long in me though. Eventually I found lots of rational Christians who could believe in both God and evolution. That made more sense to me, but it also moved me away from seeing a literal interpretation of the Bible as essential for my faith. My fling with Fundamentalism gave me some insight into what it's like to hold to a belief that goes against the opinion of the majority. I remember having a kind of disdain for non-believers, for the unsaved masses who passively accepted the science they were taught in school while ignoring God's Truth. I realized 'majority rule' was not a trustworthy principle. People think, 'if millions believe it, it must be true! Surely so many people can't be wrong!' I saw that this was exactly backwards. If millions of people believe an idea–that should make you suspicious!"

"Dad, it's hilarious that this super-extreme skepticism is what you learned from being a Creationist!"

"Totally. Thinking about it in meme terms, you could say that we humans tend to regard popularity as a measure of veracity. The more people believe a meme, the more easily it spreads through a population. Even though repetition is an inefficient way of learning, on a massive scale it works. You would think this would make people careful about what they expose themselves to. Instead, our minds skip along innocently like Little Red Riding Hood in the forest. Think about how willingly people absorb misogynistic rap songs, violent video games, pornography, hate radio, and a slew of other powerful but harmful memes.

"So should government censor these things and allow only healthful memes? You might be surprised I don't think so. Governments claim they use censorship for the good of their people. But look at China, Iran, North Korea. They use censorship to keep out political memes they don't like and pump their people full of propaganda. Controlling the media, they repeat a false message again and again. When that message is all that people hear, people believe it."

"It's like Orwell's *1984*," said Josh. "Freedom is Slavery. Ignorance is Strength. Newspeak. In the book, the government seeks total control of the thoughts of its citizens by manipulating language so that they could only think what the government wants them to. But you know, Dad, I don't think *1984* could happen today. The Internet, texting and cellphone videos are making it impossible for governments to monopolize people's memes anymore."

"You're right. I think the Internet is creating an amazing shift in people's beliefs. But the variety of opinions and experiences the Web and modern media offers doesn't mean we aren't in danger of being controlled by dangerous memes. Big Brother may not be oppressing us. He might be entertaining us into submission instead."

We could see Marita and Bastian just ahead on the trail. They were walking surprisingly slowly. We caught up to them with ease. They moved to the side of the path. Bastian motioned for us to go ahead.

"I'm feeling really nauseous," Marita told us, her face grey, her voice flat. It was clear the altitude was getting to her. "Please you go ahead. I'm not much for talking."

"But look," said Fred cheerfully, "you can see our camp for the night from here!"

He pointed to where the lava plateau sloped up to a gentle hilltop.

"Where?" We said in an eager chorus.

"You see the green ranger hut?" he pointed again.

We scanned the grey and black landscape. I could barely make out a tiny pinpoint of green. Looking around, the plateau seemed to spread as far back from where we had come as it did forward towards our destination.

Josh pulled out his camera again and then zoomed in on the green dot on the distant hill.

"See that little green hut? That over there is the littlest greenest most beautiful hut that ever was built on Kilimanjaro, and we're going to be there soon! Oh, little green hut, you're so beautiful. Oh little green hut come to us! We believe in you!"

Marita cracked a smile.

We offered to keep pace with our friends, but they insisted we go on ahead.

"So, back to beliefs," I picked up our conversation where we left off. "You remember John Milton, the author of *Paradise Lost*?"

"Sure, from English class," said Josh. "Why? Does this place remind you of Hell?"

"No, that's not it. It's about what we were talking about earlier–censorship. Milton was firmly against censorship, which sounds surprising coming from such a puritanical Calvinist. He thought it was important to expose people to ideas that were sinful. Why? Because this exposure helped people learn how to discern the good from the bad. In choosing the good, they developed moral character. In meme terms, his argument would have been that allowing exposure to bad memes strengthens people's resistance to them, and improves their ability to consciously select good memes."

"Like getting inoculated from a virus?"

"Yes! What Milton was pointing to was our ability to develop mental filters that help us decide which beliefs to accept and which to filter out. We can use these filters so that we are more resistant to memes which could otherwise be implanted by propaganda or sheer repetition..."

"Wait, Dad, this reminds me of something," Josh interrupted. "Magic Cards. You know the game, right? Well, a while ago the creators of Magic Cards answered online a question they often get from fans: 'Why do you sometimes introduce new cards into the game that are lame and lousy?' Everybody knows these cards suck, and they are real disappointed when they get one in a booster pack. So why don't the makers only put out new cards that are good? Their answer was that bad cards are necessary in order for there to be good cards. If they only created new cards that were good, then these cards would have to be better than the old ones already in play. The old cards would then become the bad cards, and the new cards would have to get more and more supercharged each new edition. This would create a spiral that would eventually make all the old cards next to worthless. So it's better if they don't start doing that. Just make some new cards powerful and others lousy to keep the game in balance."

"And to help players improve their skills of discrimination?" I added.

"Yes. That's what's really important in building a good playing deck. Not just getting good cards, but knowing how the cards play together. Sometimes an advanced player can even discover a unique strength in a weak card when it's combined with other cards."

"This is a great metaphor, Josh. It's possible to think of the beliefs we acquire from all the memes out there as like building our own deck of Magic Cards. Perhaps, if we are aware, we can consciously choose which memes we will believe in. Certainly, I've changed a lot of cards in my deck in my lifetime, more than once. Sure, I was a Bible-believing Fundamentalist in my early twenties. But in my fifties, I can cleanly say I have discarded many memes I once believed. What about you? Can you think of a time when you consciously changed one of your beliefs?

"Oh yeah. I learned something from Mom that made me decide to change something pretty major."

I have to admit that at this point I felt a sharp twinge in my chest. Josh's father is a philosopher-author who has travelled the world, delved deep into several spiritual traditions, met with mystic yogis and Tibetan masters. But when Josh thinks about a major change in his beliefs, what springs to his mind is something he learned from his mother.

"Mom gets so worried and anxious, her emotions really wind her up, and then nothing calms her down. I realized that's how I was during my relationship with Tiffani and her and my breakup. It was always so intense. When we were together, everything was all rainbows and butterflies. When we were apart, it was like, all thunderstorms and, and, dead puppies."

"I remember how hard that breakup was for you."

"Yeah. Can we stop for a minute? I need to rest."

We sat on some lava boulders as Josh continued.

"It took me a long time to get over that relationship. I mean, sure, at sixteen a year together is like a decade in teenager years. But when it was over, I realized I didn't have to be living in those extremes of happy or sad. So I decided I would just keep a baseline emotion of who I am, let other emotions come and go. Whatever happens, I just bring myself back to that baseline."

"So you wanted to stop being so emotionally reactive to events, like being tossed on the waves. Instead you found a way to keep in touch with your depths, that inner ocean that doesn't change with events. That's pretty cool."

"So when Susie left Baltimore last month to move out west, it was a totally different experience for me. I miss her. But I'm not devastated. We talk on the phone, and we both admit we will probably move on to other relationships in the future. But who knows right now what is going to happen? So I'm okay with things as they are."

"Yeah, I can see that's a pretty major shift for you. Hey, are you all right?"

Josh had closed his eyes and bent forward. He was pressing his forehead with both hands.

"My headache's getting worse. It's pounding now. When I walk, I can feel the blood throbbing in my skull with each step."

Fred, who had gone ahead, walked back to join us.

"Joshua, how you feeling?" he said.

"I'm okay. Just a headache."

Fred looked Josh up and down. He furrowed his brow and tightened his lips.

"Hmmm. You drink more water," he said.

I pulled out a water bottle and handed to Josh. Fred turned to me.

"You have pills?"

I shook my head. I didn't like taking pills unless absolutely necessary. I knew that Diamox, the only approved medicine for altitude sickness, merely treated the symptoms. I had thought it would be better to know just how your body is reacting, rather than mask a medical problem. Was that really the right decision? I watch closely as Josh drank and wiped his lips. He closed his eyes and winced.

"I'll be okay. I just need to rest a few minutes."

"It takes time to adjust," Fred said in a soothing voice. "We climbed a lot today. You drink, have a good sleep tonight, no problem. *Pole, pole. Hakuna matata.*"

The sun was behind us and dropping fast. It cast long shadows on the plateau ahead. The temperature was starting to fall, too. Fortunately, we were not more than a kilometer away from camp. We could see the hut clearly now. It stood on a rocky outcropping next to a fenced-off weather station. At 3,850 meters,

Shira 2 Camp was more than a kilometer higher than Big Tree Camp. We had pushed our bodies hard today. It should have come as no surprise that symptoms of altitude sickness were kicking in. Josh fell to the rear of our trio, his eyes to the ground. I didn't want to tax him with any more conversation. We walked in silence, picking our way over and around large lava formations that had been sculpted into intricate, abstract shapes by hundreds of thousands of years of wind and rain. It looked like a Chinese rock garden built on a monumental scale.

I asked Fred about his family. He told me more about the farm where he was raised in Tanga, near the coast. They grew vegetables for food, and maize to sell in the markets. He said he goes back to help when he's not guiding. Even during the two climbing seasons each year, he only works about two weeks a month, as there are more guides than trekking parties.

"You have children?" I asked.

"One son, Colin. He's six years old."

"So he stays with your wife while you are guiding?"

"No, his mother and I never married. She works as a nurse in a hospital in Dar es Salaam. Colin goes to boarding school in Tanga.

"Does she visit often?"

"No. She and I don't get along." He paused, seeming eager to redirect the conversation. "My sister lives near the school. She keeps an eye on the boy. It's a good school. Lutheran."

"Is it expensive?"

"Yes, $1,200 a year. I could never afford it. But there is a Lutheran donor who is paying Colin's fees."

"So he's lucky, just like you were," I said.

Fred laughed.

Jeez, I thought. A good education is out of reach for the child of a mountain guide and a nurse? At our hotel in Moshi I had met a French teacher who was working with local public school teachers on improving their teaching methods. She told me they only know how to teach by repetition.

"The teacher yells, 'Good morning, class!' and they yell back, 'Good morning, teacher!' " she told me, visibly frustrated. "It goes on like that, but they don't learn the meaning of anything they are saying. There are a hundred kids in a class. No books, no paper to write on. The parents have to buy chalk. They pay all kinds of school fees, so it's not really free. And often the teachers don't bother to show up."

The Frenchwoman told me that she was introducing the Tanzanian teachers to modern learning techniques such as using games and problem-solving, methods that were much more effective than mindless repetition, which may work for learning a song, but is not the best way to learn the memes of a second language.

"Colin's lucky to get a good education," I said to Fred. "I hope you get to spend time with him when you are not on the mountain."

Fred hesitated. "Yes, I do see him sometimes."

"It's really important for a boy to know his father." I said. I glanced back at Josh, dragging along behind us. "So when Colin's a grown man, like Josh, you can take him up Kilimanjaro."

Fred grinned at me. "That's a good idea!"

He said it with such emphasis it seemed like the first time the thought had occurred to him.

We reached the base of the hill called Shira 2. All we had to do was scramble up the slope to our campsite. We had walked seven hours our second day on the trail and we were thoroughly exhausted. The sun hung low in the sky as we staggered to the top, legs wobbly, faces stinging from a full day in the sun and wind. The camp had only a handful of tents pitched on it. The ground was rocky with few smooth patches and sparse vegetation except for a little grove of Scotch thistles with prickly, purple flowers, sheltered behind the green metal hut. White-necked ravens hopped about. They were large, jet-black birds with markings that looked like white shirt collars. Josh didn't say anything. He looked pale and in pain. We followed Fred into the green hut to sign our names in the book.

Exiting the hut, we turned and saw to the southwest the sunset lighting the tops of the clouds below. They bunched up against the jagged pinnacles that ran up the south side of Shira's long-extinct cone. It created a peculiar optical illusion, as if the clouds beneath us were an ocean whose soft, rolling waves crashed against the cliffs of a distant, rocky shore–the shore of our sky island. Turning around, to the northeast I saw Kilimanjaro, bathed in pink light. We had walked fifteen kilometers towards it since it first came into view that morning.

"It seems much, much bigger now," said Josh.

"But not much closer," I added.

The sun went down. Darkness dropped suddenly, as if someone had switched off the light. Strong winds blew in, bringing sub-zero cold down from the sky. An hour earlier we had been wearing shorts and t-shirts. We found our tent, dove inside and quickly changed into our poly-fill jackets, fleeces and long underwear, and still we were shivering. In the dinner tent we clutched our mugs of tea tight for the warmth they brought to our fingers. I thought to myself: this is just 3,850 meters. We have more than two vertical kilometers up still to go. How much colder can it get?

At dinnertime, Josh could barely eat. He managed a bowl of vegetable soup and half a plate of rice.

"Friend? You okay, friend?" Sully asked, his voice full of genuine concern. "Drink water!"

Josh went to bed ahead of me. I sat in the dinner tent and wrote in my journal by the light of my head lamp. Finished, I stepped outside into a moonless sky filled with stars. I craned my neck back and soaked in the Milky Way and the unfamiliar constellations of the southern sky. It was hard to remember we were just 300 kilometers south of the equator, that just off this plateau lions roared and elephants roamed. I shivered and rubbed my hands. It was too cold to stand still. By my watch it was not yet eight p.m., but there was nothing left to do but sleep. Josh was inside his bag when I entered the tent. He said his headache was no better. I dug around in my pack for some Advil. He washed the pills down with cold water.

"At least I'm so exhausted I know I'm going to sleep. Oh boy! Can't wait for oblivion."

I smiled in the dark. Even in pain, he could crack a joke.

Sully called out softly at the tent flaps. I unzipped, and he handed us two of our hard plastic water bottles, filled to the top with hot water. He told us to put them inside our sleeping bags. I was afraid they might leak and wet our bags. However it was too cold to argue, so I accepted the bottles and did as he said. It was the most exquisite sensation, this hard plastic radiating heat against my shivering body. I clutched the bottle close to my chest. It almost burned.

"Josh, I think I'm in love."

"Oh, welcome, water bottle!" Josh said, and promptly fell asleep.

I closed my eyes, so glad to be warm and lying still.

Sleep would not come. There was a hard, sore spot in the center of my chest, beneath the surface where the bottle was hot against me. It felt old and familiar. Josh was suffering because of my decision not to bring altitude pills. I felt the spot with my fingertips. A moment came back to me. Josh was three years old. His mother and I had only been on our every-other-week custody arrangement for a month or so. I had come to her house to pick him up at the start of my week. At the door her father told me she had taken Josh to see the doctor. He had a fever and had been vomiting. When I got to the doctor's, I found him crying in his mother's arms. After his examination, Josh's mother insisted she was going to take him back home with her. He needed his mother, she told me, and she did not care about a court-ordered schedule. I called my lawyer on the doctor's office phone (this was before cell service). My lawyer called her lawyer. Her lawyer called the doctor's office and he talked to her while Josh whimpered and clung to her like a baby chimp. Her face flushed with anger and confusion at her attorney's words. She hung up, looking anguished. I hardened myself, clenching my jaw and fists, pressing down on my weak feelings as she started to cry.

"Is there any medical reason why Josh shouldn't go home with his father?" I asked the doctor.

"No reason he can't go home with either parent," she said curtly. The poor woman was clearly distressed and annoyed that her office had become ground zero in a custody battle.

I plucked Josh from his mother's arms. As she released him he started to scream, clawing the air for her. I felt like a god-damn kidnapper. I walked out of the office and quickly down the hall and he calmed down. I felt terrified. Had I traumatized him? What would happen if his fever got worse out at the farm where I lived? But I knew with conviction that if I let his mother keep him this once, I would forever be the lesser parent. Every sniffle would serve as an excuse for her to keep him from me.

"I'm his father. I'm good enough, I'm good enough." I repeated to myself like a mantra as I carried him to the car, and he dropped into an exhausted sleep in my arms.

The winter I was in third grade, five bad boys used to beat me up every day at recess. I always had my hand up in class: pick me, teacher, pick me! And so the bad boys picked me too. The beatings had a ritualistic quality to them, like something out of Lord of the Flies. First they would hunt me through the crowded school yard. They would grab me and march me to the far corner where there was a low wall. Two of them—the guards—would hold me by the arms, one on each side. The others would take turns climbing the wall, each positioning himself right behind me, then jumping down and knocking me to the ground. The guards would haul me back to my feet, and the ritual would be repeated again and again, until the bell rang. Then they would run inside. I would wipe the tears and snot and cinders from my face and go back to class.

I used to beg Mrs. Zabinski to let me stay indoors to clean the blackboard and bang the dust out of the chalk erasers. Usually she would send me out to meet my fate. I never told her what was happening to me. I suppose she thought me lazy for wanting to skip recess. The teachers monitoring the schoolyard never seemed to notice. My tormentors were strategic, going to the far corner and crowding around me so no one outside the circle could see. I told my best friend, Sean, and he tried to stop them. So they hauled him to the corner and jumped on him too. I didn't blame him for avoiding me at recess after that. I figured somehow I deserved this. After a while, I would just march silently between the guards and take the beatings with as little crying as possible.

My parents were concerned when I said I didn't want to go to school any more. I broke down and told them what was happening to me.

"Do you know which one is the leader?" my father asked with a curious excitement.

I nodded, "Wayne Merriman."

Relief flooded my little body that my parents were going to do something. Perhaps the police would now arrest Wayne Merriman?

"Next time, you pick the leader out, and you mark him," my father instructed vehemently. "Break his nose. Cut his lip."

He put up his arms and demonstrated how to jab. It was as if he wanted to watch the fight.

"But Daddy, they hold my arms. There's too many of them."

"Mark the leader. Then the rest of them will leave you alone."

So I endured the beatings, ashamed to talk any more to my father about my failure to mark Wayne Merriman. When I look back, I can't believe I suffered such cruelty with so little complaint. I think I must have misinterpreted my father's code of corporal punishment. "You are being spanked because you broke the rules" translated in my young brain as: "If someone is inflicting pain on you, then you must have done something to deserve it." So the beatings were my punishment for *making the bad boys feel dumb. I'm pretty sure I got that part right. Looking back, the one thing I like is the fact that it never occurred to that nine-year-old boy to stop raising his hand in class.*

Chapter Four

To Lava Tower

Day Three: to Barranco Wall (3,976 meters)
11 kilometers

"Day three is Acclimatization Day," Fred told us before we went to bed.

He said we would trek right to the base of Kibo, Kilimanjaro's main volcano cone, then climb up a massive tower of lava to 4,600 meters. After that, we would descend into a valley. This climb and retreat would help us get used to the altitude. The top of the tower was still 1,400 meters (about a vertical mile) below the summit, but it would give Fred a good gauge of any serious AMS symptoms that might hit us later. The original Lemosho trekking route used to run from Lava Tower directly to the summit. But that pathway traverses the so-called Western Breach, a collapsed section of the volcano rim where rockslides are frequent. Fred explained that the government temporarily closed it a few years earlier after a slide killed several climbers. Now, trekkers come tantalizingly close to the summit along this route before they are obliged to back off. From Lava Tower we would hike around the south flank of the volcano and then across to the eastern face for the final ascent.

Josh's headache had not gotten any better. The Advil had not helped, though he did sleep through the night. I knew because I heard him snore. My insomnia–a mild AMS symptom–lasted until dawn. I felt surprisingly rested just from lying still for ten hours, cuddling my water bottle and listening to the wind whip the sides of our tent.

At breakfast I slurped my warm millet porridge while Josh

chewed listlessly on a limp, rolled-up pancake. After a few small bites he pushed it aside. He didn't touch his little red hot dogs either. Sully returned. He looked at Josh's plate, wrinkled his brow and shook his head.

"Friend, Joshua, you eat?" he said with in gentle tones like a coaxing mother.

"I'm just not hungry. Headache." Josh pointed a finger to his head.

"Ohhh…You drink lots water. Drink, okay?"

"Yeah, okay Sully. Thanks"

"He's so sweet to me," Josh said with a slight smile, his eyes following our waiter as he left the tent. He paused, then looked back at me. "Dad, do you think I'm going to make it?"

"Yeah," I nodded earnestly. "We've got three days to acclimatize before the summit. Is it any better now?

"Nope. About the same."

"On a scale of one to ten?"

"It's an eight."

I thought of all the times when this guy was a kid, when I had the right pills or took him to the doctor or at least could just hold him in my arms and reassure him that everything would be okay. It was hard to remember those times when facing this new man who was already half an inch taller than me, the beard on his face coming in, just as mine was after a few days on the mountain. I still wanted to make it all better. But there was nothing I could do. And now we were going to spend the day hiking 800 meters higher.

"Good morning, brothers!" Fred pushed through the tent flaps and greeted us cheerfully. "Today we are walking to the moon! This part of Kilimanjaro, almost nothing grows. It's like a desert. So we call it 'Moonland.' Please remember to take a lot of water, because there will be no more water where we stop for lunch. It's important you drink a lot. Even if you don't sweat, your body loses so much moisture."

A handsome, dark-skinned man with weathered features, doubtless a sign of his many trips up the mountain, stood waiting by our tent, hands on hips.

"*Jambo!*" he said in a deep voice. "My name is Benjamin. I am head porter. Please, your bags!"

He gestured to the mouth of the tent, gracefully. Inside, our bags, which we had packed up earlier, were visible through the open outer flap and mosquito netting. It seemed there was a certain etiquette that prevented porters from entering our tent, even if only to remove our luggage. I realized our crew was waiting to dismantle our tent and begin the daily race to beat us to the next camp so that it would be all set up when we arrived. We pulled out the bags and handed them over. Benjamin smiled. Josh and I shouldered our day packs. As we started up the trail behind Fred, we heard Benjamin's voice once more, summoning the men to their task.

The path we started on was different. It was no longer dirt. There was nothing organic left in it. It seemed powdery, just pulverized volcanic dust. The only living things on the ground were sparse tufts of grass, the odd bunch of white "Everlasting" flowers, and patches of lichen, white or bright orange, encrusting the lava rocks. The only birds we saw were the white-necked ravens, which fed on carrion and scraps left by trekkers. Once we saw vultures spiraling high overhead.

Because it was still freezing cold when we started out, we had worn thermal underwear under our trousers. But the hot morning sun quickly cut through the thin, dry air. Soon we were sweating. We stripped down to our t-shirts and unzipped our pant legs at the thighs, a nifty feature of trekking trousers that converts them into shorts. With our black silk long johns underneath, we looked ludicrous (Or so I thought. The following winter I found myself in Paris, where the stylish young women were wearing woolen hot-pants over black pantyhose as the sophisticated meme of the season. It turns out Josh and I were ahead of the fashion trend).

The porters soon passed us on the trail, one by one, charging by with loads on their shoulders or balanced on their heads. We heard them exchange greetings with Fred. "*Mambo?*" One would say. "*Jambo!*" The other would reply.

"*Mambo?*" I called to one of them as he passed.

"*Poa!*" He said with a laugh.

I asked Fred to explain.

"Instead of *Jambo*, you can say *Poa*! Which means 'cool!' " he told us.

Fred started singing the Swahili song about Kilimanjaro again. We practiced it over and over. I sensed Fred's real purpose was to help Josh take his mind off his headache. He was too whacked to sing much, but would always chime in enthusiastically with the final line: "Kilimanjaro, *Hakuna matata*!"

By midmorning we caught up again with Marita and Bastian. Marita said her nausea had gotten worse. She told us she had had to move slowly just to keep from vomiting. Her smile was gone. She looked down at her feet, concentrating so that she did not stumble. We eased off to match their pace, but once more they urged us to walk on ahead. We hesitated.

"She'll be all right," Bastian said in his flat Terminator voice.

"How do you know?" I asked, a bit abruptly.

He looked at me. "She took Diamox this morning."

"Is that a good idea? That just masks the symptoms."

"No," Bastian shook his head. "Diamox doesn't mask symptoms. It makes the blood more...more..."

"More acidic," panted Marita. "Acidifying the blood makes the red blood cells transfer more oxygen. It creates the good effects of acclimatization."

I looked at her skeptically.

"She works in a *hospital*." Bastian said.

We wished them good luck, and pushed on.

"You damn idiot," I cursed myself under my breath. I had

refused to get a Diamox prescription back home based on a false assumption. I felt certain I knew what was best without really doing the research. Now Josh was suffering for it.

"*Mambo!*" cried a voice behind me. It was Benjamin, with Josh's blue duffle bag on his back.

"*Poa!*" Josh returned, and Benjamin laughed.

"Benjamin, Ezekiel, Solomon, Nathaniel," I mused. "It's like climbing a mountain with the cast of the Old Testament."

"Maybe God will provide us with tablets at the top?" said Josh. "Diamox, I hope."

"Ouch," I said.

"What was that story, Dad? I remember it from when you read the Bible to me when I was in middle school. A father and son, they were climbing a mountain."

"The story of Abraham and Isaac, from Genesis. Not a great father-son bonding tale, actually."

"Yeah, I remember now. They forgot to bring a sheep with them or something…"

"Um, yeah," I said, "Isaac keeps wondering where the sacrificial lamb is. Abraham tells him, 'Don't worry, son, the Lord will provide.' The kid doesn't know that God told Abraham it was not a sheep that was to be sacrificed on the mountain top. God wanted Abraham to sacrifice his only *son*. Abraham ties the boy up, raises the knife, he strikes—but, in the nick of time an angel of the Lord appears and grabs Abraham's arm. Enough, the angel says, God only wanted to test your obedience. Now God knows you love Him more than anything else…"

"This must have seriously fucked the kid up," Josh laughed. "'Oh, it's your lucky day, Isaac! My invisible friend Jehovah, you know, the one who told me I should kill you? He changed His mind! So I'm not going to cut your throat after all!' 'That's awesome, Dad! Why not untie me, and maybe we can have another fun adventure like this some *other* day!'"

We laughed.

"I am so glad I gave you a good Biblical education when you were young," I said.

"Yep. You sure inoculated me well from those Bible memes!"

"But you know, Josh, the Bible is a great example of how individual beliefs cluster together over hundreds, sometimes thousands of years, coagulating into sets of interconnected, self-reinforcing memes. These giant meme clusters are called memeplexes. This includes systems of religion, science, philosophy, morality, ethnic identity, nationalism, and political ideology, just to name a few.

"For example, Christianity contains this set of memes that all fit together: Original Sin: every person is born in sin. Hell: sinners go to a place of eternal torment. Redemption: through Jesus, God forgives repentant sinners. Baptism: through this rite, sinners are washed clean. Faith: believe that Jesus is the Son of God, and this forgiveness will work for you. Obedience: Obey and support the church as God's instrument on earth. You can see how these memes mesh to create a single congruent system that spreads and sustains itself. In fact, when I was an Evangelical, I really believed I had to tell everybody about Jesus to save them from hell. Since those days, I've studied the history of Original Sin. This doctrine, which I had thought was a bedrock part of Christianity, was actually constructed by St. Augustine in the 4th Century A.D. At the time it was only one of many competing and widely differing ideas about sin and the meaning of Jesus's death. Some memes won out and became Church dogma. The memes that were rejected became heresy. Heretics who believed in the losing memes or refused to change their minds were excommunicated and sometimes killed.

"The idea of belief systems as memeplexes helped me to see that they don't have to be true or good or even ethical in order to persist and spread. They just have to successfully replicate and stick in people's minds. Maybe their rules were easy to remember and follow. Maybe they had rituals, often repeated, that induced in believers strong emotions, whether ecstasy or fear. Maybe they had successful propagation strategies, like preaching or catchy hymns. Or maybe the memes worked together to create a system that was really good at getting rid of competing memes. If you can say, "My God is the one true God, all the others are false. Believe like we do or else in God's name we must kill you..."

"That's pretty persuasive."

"Exactly. The idea of absolute truth with a capital 'T' is a very potent meme. When we believe something is True, we tend to cease evaluating it against alternatives. It makes us stop thinking. People willingly die for such a truth"

"I don't get it – so do you think there is such a thing as Truth?"

"Okay, Josh, so now you have asked the million-dollar question. I spent more than a decade studying both Western and Eastern philosophy trying to answer it, and guess what? I got no final answer. Here's what makes the most sense to me though: There may be an absolute truth, but the human mind is limited and finite. It is limited by our subjective perceptions and thoughts. Our brain was forged over a few million years of evolution on the African savannah. It's great at perceiving what such a brain needs to survive. It's good at solving human sized problems, but not so good at other things, like seeing atoms and far away galaxies. Amazingly we have asked questions and invented things like microscopes and telescopes to help us see these things so far from the human realm. But I doubt we will ever be able to build a device that tells us absolutely whether or not something is True.

"So to me 'truth' is really about finding good rough guides that are congruent with my experience. Does this belief fit with all my other beliefs and experiences at this level of perception? Does it help me accurately predict what is going to happen next? When a belief fits neatly into a person's internalized belief system, it feels like a piece of a puzzle locking into place. That's congruence. We experience congruence not just intellectually, but as a bodily sense of satisfaction. It just feels right. And when it feels right, we think that we are right. The error people make is in thinking that this internal sense of 'feels right' equals 'Truth.' When we make this mistake, we become attached to our beliefs as if they are absolutes, and rigidly resist change. Like the Church with Galileo, we feel threatened by new ideas or observations. We want to attack or expel them. But if we can keep in mind that our beliefs are only rough guides, we can create space to explore and evaluate new information."

"What about meme theory then? Is that True?" asked Josh.

"Of course not, not in any absolute sense. It's a good rough guide that explains a lot about the mind and human culture work. The fact is no one has ever seen a meme."

"I thought you said that everything was a meme, like axes and computers?"

"No, strictly speaking, memes are ideas. Axes and computers are the vehicles that help convey the idea to others. A meme itself exists in our brain as an electrochemical firing pattern of millions of nerve cells that can replicate itself. I picture it like a complex string of Christmas tree lights turning on and off in our heads."

"Or like a computer file," Josh jumped in. "It's made up of a code of electrical charges, but you can open and store that code it as many times as you want."

"Yeah, good analogy. I imagine someday scientists will be able to map out neural firing patterns and determine if any of these patterns correlate with certain ideas. They have already discovered that stimulating certain parts of the brain causes people to have very specific, vivid memories. So I think it's possible we will see a meme one day."

We had begun climbing up a steep and rocky ridge. We took a pause for water, and Josh told me the story about the power of belief. A friend in his university theater classes was a strict Orthodox Jew. She had been forced to withdraw from the acting program because her faith forbade her from performing during

Shabbat–Friday night or Saturday, which is of course when most student shows were held. What aggravated Josh was that there were exceptions to some of the strict rules she had to follow, but not others.

"One example that drove me nuts was that she could not turn on a TV on the Shabbat. But if somebody else turned it on, she could watch it. It just seemed so arbitrary. Another thing, she was not permitted to be touched by a man, but if they were in a scene together, and the scene called for contact, then she could let him touch her. I asked if I could hug her if only our clothing touched. She said no, that was not permitted. So we came up with a system: I would hug my back pack then pass it to her, and she would hug it too."

Her beliefs came at a huge cost to her chosen professional career. Josh said she had accepted it, though, and was going to find other ways to pursue her dreams as an actress.

Our trail took us up and down steep valleys and hills as we approached Kilimanjaro's main peak. Embedded in some of the raw boulders we could see what looked like little white grains of rice, hundreds of them. Fred told us these were porphyry crystals, formed inside the volcano itself during the eruption and immediate cooling of the lava. He said this was a rare type, found in only three places in the world. Later, I checked the Web and verified he was right. This was rhomb porphyry, found only on Kilimanjaro and the Rift Valley, Mount Erebus in Antarctica, and Oslo Graben in Norway.

We stopped to rest in the shade of a giant boulder in the bottom of a valley. Fred pointed out hoof prints just off the trail.

"Buffalo," he said.

"Why would a massive creature like an African buffalo climb all this way up a rocky gulch, past 4,000 meters?" I asked. "For the view?"

"To eat lichen," Fred said.

"Must be pretty tasty," said Josh, rubbing his temples.

"It's good for them. Like medicine," Fred said.

He looked around, then gestured to the ground in front of the boulder.

"A porter died here last year," he said. "It rained. He did not have a spare set of clothing. He fell behind and no one noticed. He died of the cold. The government is much stricter now, making sure porters all have proper equipment."

It was a somber moment. It's one thing to risk death on a spectacular adventure. Another to be left behind when you fall, just doing your job, doing what it takes to feed your family, and to have no one notice. You spend your last hours alone in the dark and cold, growing numb, knowing all too well nobody will come to your rescue. We said a silent prayer and moved on.

By midday we reached the base of Lava Tower. At 4,600 meters, this was our highest point of the trek so far. It's a huge chimney of fused basalt lava about 100 meters (300 feet) high that sits like a giant wart on the mountain's southwestern shoulder. At the base of the tower some groups had already pitched their tents for the night. Scores of porters were milling around setting up camp. Others lay back on the rocks and cracked jokes. I thought about these men who could fly along the trail at twice our speed, and now looked like they didn't have a care in the world. This must be incredibly tough work, at least as tough as any physical labor I've every done, and that's not counting the altitude. I couldn't do their job, and yet they were each doing it for me for about $10 a day. And this, by all counts, was a great wage in a county with a per capita income of about $500 per year. This was development tourism working well, and still it seemed far from an even transaction.

We threw off our day packs. At our request, the porters had set up the lunch table outside today. It seemed crazy to be sitting in a tent when we had Kilimanjaro as our backdrop. The blue table cloth had been anchored in place by the various condiment jars so lunch wouldn't take flight in the strong wind. We sat on our folding chairs, sipped our little boxes of orange juice, nibbled on crumbly biscuits and stared up at the world's highest volcano, directly in front of us, while we waited for lunch to be served.

"Welcome carrot soup!" Sully announced.

I sucked up the broth hungrily. Josh shot another video.

"This is the most amazing carrot soup ever made! And where else do you find a restaurant with a view from the roof of the world?"

He clicked off the camera. Suddenly, the energy drained from his body. He slumped in his chair.

"Headache back?" I asked.

"When I was walking, my head jarred with every step, like someone was pounding a nail into my skull. When I sat down I felt better. But that only lasted a minute. Now it hurts all through my head and I feel sick."

He put a few spoonfuls of soup into his mouth. He looked up and saw me scrutinizing him with a worried look. He picked up a biscuit and slowly mashed it against his face without opening his mouth, making cookie-monster growling sounds. Crumbs fell all over his lap and the table. He gave a half-hearted laugh.

"Okay, so that's a good sign," I said. "Unless you are in fact losing all coordination."

"Could I get some more Advil?"

I handed him three. He swallowed the blue pills. His head sank to his chest. Tears ran down his face from behind his sunglasses.

"Dad, what if I can't make it?"

"We've still got three days to acclimatize," I said. "You just need time to get used to it. We'll be going down soon. I'm sure it will ease up."

That's what I said. What I felt like doing was holding him in my arms and whispering, "There, there, it'll be all right. I'll make it stop hurting." But it was not, and I could not, and he was not a child I could comfort any more.

When Fred joined us he took one look at Josh and announced that we had acclimatized enough for the day. We were not going to climb to the top of Lava Tower. Instead we would immediately head downhill. The camp for the night was a good 500 meters lower than our current altitude. Getting lower would help reduce the headache, he assured us. Fred unstrapped the walking poles he had been carrying for Josh. This would give Josh some extra balance while we were descending.

"Tonight you take some Diamox, Josh," Fred said.

"But Fred," I blurted out, exasperated and ashamed, "I *told* you, I didn't bring any altitude pills."

"I have some pills," he said calmly. "A client from another trip did not use them. She left them with me."

Josh looked up hopefully.

"Oh, that's wonderful," I said, flooded with relief. "Do you suppose Josh could take one now?'

"No. It's dangerous to take pills at high altitude. You never know what is going to happen. ASM can get very serious. So when we get lower, then it will be okay. So now we just go down, *pole, pole*. Josh, I will carry your pack."

"No Fred, I can manage," said Josh.

Fred picked up Josh's day pack and strapped it on top of his own. "*Hakuna matata*, Josh" he said with a grin.

"Thanks, Fred. You take good care of us," Josh said.

The trip downhill from Lava Tower was rough. We worked our way slowly along a winding and treacherous drop to the bottom of a steep valley. Josh moved slowly, concentrating on each step, forcing himself to stay in motion, steadying himself with the poles to avoid slipping on the loose shale. Fred and I would turn and stop to wait for him. Now and then he would skid. Once or twice he slipped and fell on his backside. Not a hard jolt, fortunately. The path was so steep he just fell into a sitting position. But I knew this must be shooting pain through his head each time it happened. It was excruciating to watch.

When we reached the bottom of the valley we heard a sound like rolling thunderclaps. A cloud of dust appeared far above us on the slope of the volcano.

"Rockslide," said Fred, shielding his eyes with both hands to look up at it.

I could see what looked like small pebbles bouncing down the side of the volcano, careening like billiard balls into the top of the valley through which we were climbing. These tiny pebbles were a few kilometers away. Were they going to roll all the way down to where we stood? I looked around. Giant boulders littered the valley floor, some big as cars, some big as houses. Do we run? Do we hide? I watched, transfixed. I had to keep thinking of them as pebbles to keep myself from panicking. So this was why the government closed the Western Breach trail to the top.

These frequent slides, I later learned, were the result of a 'freeze-thaw' process. Subzero nights and hot days make the top centimeters of the rock face contract and expand, creating tiny fissures. It's the same process that creates potholes on city streets. Water gets into the cracks. It freezes then thaws, again and again, forming wedges of ice that widen the cracks with each cycle. Like a slow-motion jackhammer, the process fragments the outer shell of the volcano, eventually popping loose giant boulders just like the ones rolling our way now. It's a fascinating geological phenomenon to observe, though at the time I was more interested in whether or not we were going to be crushed to death. I took my cue from Fred, who watched closely, calmly, and in no apparent rush to escape to higher ground. I couldn't tell if this meant we were in no danger, or if we were in danger, but could not escape no matter how fast we ran, so *Hakuna matata*.

The dust and the rocks eventually settled in place well above us. The thunder halted. Fred picked up his pack again and led us forward without a word.

We climbed up the far side of the valley, hand over hand up a steep slope. Fred put Josh in the middle between us. He didn't want to talk, didn't want to stop. He kept going, his face pinched, mouth tight. Over the crest, the trail dropped just as steeply once more, making the descent slow and tortuous.

We passed a strapping young Danish man and his Tanzanian guide, taking a rest. The guide was carrying the young man's pack (emblazoned with the red flag and white cross of Denmark). The Dane, seated on a rock, held his head in his hands.

"How's it going?" said Josh.

"Bad," the Dane groaned. "You?"

"Terrible. But we are all on our way down now. It's sure to get better."

The Dane smiled feebly. Josh turned to go. He hesitated, turned back, and gave the guy a big hug.

"Good luck!" said Josh.

"I feel like part of a club now," Josh told me. "Brotherhood of the Splitting Headaches."

The joke was a good sign. Another few hundred meters down, he was moving quicker, his head up.

"Dad, I've got a question," he said, his voice suddenly upbeat. "Mythologies are memeplexes, too, right? Like the ancient Greeks?"

"Of course," I said. I could hardly believe he was bringing the conversation back to memes. He must be feeling better. Or succumbing to delirium. "What we call 'mythology' is really just the religion of other people. We commonly use 'myth' to mean 'something other people believe that we know is not true,' like urban legends. In fact, the real characteristic of a mythology is that it explains the world in a coherent narrative. A mythology tells stories about how the world came to be the way it is, and why we are the way we are. In this sense, every religious system is a mythology."

Josh described in detail a mythology-based video game he enjoyed playing, *God of War*, in which the player takes on the identity of a man bent on revenging himself against the Greek Gods. He kills them off, one by one.

"So it's the thrill of being a mortal man," I said, "and killing the immortals?"

"And he's also having this fling with Aphrodite at the same time. He kills a God, then goes and screws the Goddess."

"Well, I guess the makers of the game know how to hook their target audience," I said grimly.

"No kidding," laughed Josh. "My point was, you were saying how religious belief systems were memeplexes. Wouldn't each video game be a memeplex, too?"

"I guess so," I said slowly. "The idea never occurred to me."

"Sure, each game creates its own world, defined by hundreds of memes. The player has to figure out for himself the rules of the game. He has to learn the strategies and skills to guide him along the way."

"Ah, I see," I said. "A game's internal coherent reality is its mythology, just like any religion."

We had to break off talking for a few minutes where the path dropped so vertically it felt as if we were scrambling down a dry waterfall. One or two quick steps could put you out of control and into a tumble. It put strain on a completely different set of leg muscles. My knees ached. Fred positioned himself at key spots and held our hands as we clambered down. I needed his support. I felt like a ninety-year old man negotiating my way slowly down a fire escape. I tried to apply what Josh had told me about the Alexander Technique, to glide down the slope with as little waste of energy as possible, but I could not stop my legs from shaking.

The valley into which we descended had a silver stream running down the center of it, bringing back plant life that we had not seen all day on our long walk through Moonland. For the first time we encountered a weird, new kind of tree, the giant groundsel. Fred said was called the "Kilimanjaro Tree," because it only grew here and on a few other mountains in East Africa.

These trees were shaped rather like giant cactuses, growing up to about five meters (fifteen feet) tall, with huge branches that curved upwards from a single trunk at odd angles. The trunk and branches were covered with a thick mat of dead leaves. It looked almost like they were wearing puffy fur coats. Green, living leaves sprouted from the tops of the branches in big, fan-like, circular tufts. Some of these tufts had a straggly, flower-covered spike sticking up from the center towards the sky, like peculiar, whimsical antennae.

"They look too wacky to be real," I said to Josh.

"Like something out of Dr. Seuss," he replied.

The small plain at the bottom of the distant valley was studded with hundreds of these crazy Kilimanjaro trees, but also speckled with dots of bright blue, orange, green and yellow fabric. Some seventy tents were already pitched for the night. Fred explained that at this valley the Lemosho route to the summit merged with the Umbwe route. The trekkers from both trails converged here for the night, making a tent town, rather than a village. Seeing our destination gave Josh and me a final boost of energy. As the path eased off into a level walk, we picked up our pace.

As we walked I pondered these unknown and complex virtual worlds my son so effortlessly inhabited. As a teen, he had wanted to share his favorite video games with me. He would sit at my side in front of the computer and coach me through various levels. My hand-keyboard coordination was painfully slow, nowhere near fast enough for many of the tasks that came as second nature to Josh. Sometimes he would step in when I was failing and getting frustrated, and complete the task for me. I appreciated him for wanting to share what he loved. But I had not really appreciated until this moment that these imaginary worlds he navigated with such ease were meme systems poten-tially as complex as any mythological epic. I could see now that these role-play video games were very much like visual novels in which the protagonist could move about freely, discovering and exploring the landscape and characters within. How dull it must seem to gamers that a written tale has only one single pathway from beginning to end. I realized that for Josh the experience of coaching his struggling, ill-coordinated father at the keyboard must have been something akin to trying to teach an illiterate man how to read.

We strolled into the valley, flat as a dry riverbed. The weird loopy-branched trees and the angular, bright-colored tents created a perceptual clash, as if Pablo Picasso and Salvador Dali had painted the scene together on a single canvas.

Our little bowls of warm water were waiting for us beside our tent. We splashed the dust and sweat from our faces, then went straight to dinner.

"Welcome macaroni and tuna!"

Sully beckoned us to another surreal Kilimanjaro meal. I had thought perhaps this dish would mimic that old camping staple I had eaten round so many campfires in Canada: a box of Kraft noodles, a packet of cheddar cheese powder, a tin of tuna, and voila! Not so on Kilimanjaro. The noodles were served plain, like spaghetti. Onto it Sully ladled chunked tuna in an orange sauce that looked like cheese sauce but was in fact vegetable soup. The mixture looked remarkably like a bowl of vomit. But it tasted amazing: soupy and fishy and chewy with a hint of tomato and little bubbles of fat. Josh started slurping it down like a dog at his dinner bowl, the first real meal he had eaten since the potato-egg lunch the previous day.

"Sully, this is the most delicious, fabulous meal I have ever had in my life!" he said.

Sully beamed with pleasure as we helped ourselves to seconds.

After eating, we sipped our tea by the light of the mushroom-tin candelabra and talked about the day. Fred entered the tent. He held in his hand an orange prescription bottle filled with little white pills.

"Diamox?" I asked.

Fred nodded.

"Josh, how is your head?" he asked.

"Oh, I still have a headache. But compared to what I felt like at lunch, I feel like now I'm dancing in a field of buttercups."

"You should take pills," Fred said.

"Can I read the label for side effects?" I asked.

Fred handed the bottle to me.

" 'May cause drowsiness. Don't operate heavy machinery.' Hmm...Josh, you think you can operate your walking poles?"

"*Hakuna matata*," said Josh.

He mimed going spastic with invisible walking poles, stabbing and smashing into everything in the tent. Definitely, he was feeling better.

Fred turned to me. "So, give him half a pill after dinner, another half in the morning. Make sure he drinks it with lots of water."

I nodded to Fred. I had my hand on the top to pop open the bottle and break a pill in two. Wait a minute, I checked myself. The parent memes were taking over. I paused. Josh looked up at me. Our eyes met. I handed the bottle across the table to him. Yeah, he's old enough to take his own medicine.

My father called me a 'clot' when I was a child. It was a made-up word that meant stupid and clumsy. He would say it whenever he was mad at me for doing something dumb, like breaking a dish or forgetting something. It made me feel humiliated and ashamed. Sometimes he would do it just for fun. I remember walking along a beach with him and him writing with his foot "Tim is a clot," over and over in the sand in giant letters, so big I imagined it could be seen from an airplane. I ran along behind him, erasing the letters with my hands, crying for him to stop.

"Don't cry," he said, laughing, "I'm only teasing."

Chapter Five

Under the Glacier's Toe

Day Four: to Karanga Valley (3,995 meters)
5 kilometers

No doubt about it, I stank. Bacteria do not thrive at high altitudes. Theoretically, one can go a long time this high without a bath. But waking up the fourth day on Kilimanjaro with all the odors of the mountain zip-locked inside my sleeping bag with me, I knew it was time to take action. When Josh went out to visit the potty-tent, I rummaged through my duffle bag and found the special item I had been saving for just this moment. While shopping for trip supplies a month earlier, I had been thrilled to find a camping accessory that was new to me: man-sized wet wipes. Wet wipes are a parent's best friend. These little moist tissues with a slight antiseptic sting make changing diapers easy and sanitary, and can also clean a dirty face or sticky hands. But these beauties I found at REI were made for head-to-toe adult body rubdowns. Each napkin unfolded to the dimensions of a laptop keyboard. Using both sides, I found I could wash about one quarter of my carcass before the wipe turned grey and grimy. Four wipes and 10 minutes later I felt clean and fresh as the proverbial daisy.

Josh, while appreciating my change of skin color, declined to use them on himself, no matter how enthusiastically I promoted the daisy-fresh feeling. Though he did not smell as bad as I did, he looked frightful. His hair seemed to be made of solid clumps that stuck up from his scalp at odd angles like palm fronds, like some Claymation-cartoon version of himself. And he was covered with feathers. His down sleeping bag was leaking. Since he was sleeping in his fleece jacket and long johns, white tufts of down had gotten stuck in the fibers.

"Maybe I'm turning into a poofy turkey-monkey," he laughed.

His headache was gone, his appetite revived. We welcomed breakfast and he cleaned his plate. Sully beamed.

"Joshua, okay! Joshua–me–friend!" He touched Josh's arm, then his own heart, and grinned again.

The walk today would be a short one, Fred explained after breakfast, just five kilometers. But there would be a lot of steep climbing up and down at high altitude, so we would go slowly, covering about a kilometer each hour. To start, we would scale the cliff on the far side of the valley, known as the Barranco Wall, a climb of 200 meters (600 feet), straight up.

The little glacial stream flowed alongside the base of the cliff. The morning sun glistened off a thin layer of ice that covered the stream's banks. Mist rose from the ice like a translucent veil in front of the wall. As we drew near we saw that the ice had given the stepping stones in the stream a glossy sheen, making it difficult to cross without slipping and plunging ankle deep in the frigid water–not a great way to start a day's trek. Fred hopped nimbly across and then steadied each of us so that we only splashed our waterproof boots without soaking them.

Where the wall began, the trail turned into a steep switchback etched upon the rock face. We picked our way slowly over jagged chunks of lava. In some places the footpath disappeared and we had to climb straight up, one careful handhold at a time. Our conversation dropped to nothing as we struggled to keep our breath and focus on each grip. After hauling ourselves up a particularly challenging stretch, we rested on a broad ledge. We gulped water, gulped air. I was sweating profusely. Looking straight down, we saw the icy stream, just a thin, white line at the base of the wall far below us. Across the valley we watched the last of the tents coming down, the patches of colors folding up and disappearing amidst the trunks of the crazy, tufted Kilimanjaro trees. Our porters started coming up behind us, precariously balancing their heavy loads on their heads while they used both hands to pull themselves up. It was insane to watch this take place without the use of a single climbing rope. Josh and I could barely manage to haul our own asses up the cliff, let alone loaded down with groceries and gear bags. Nathaniel appeared, carrying a load wrapped in canvas on his head that I guessed must have been our toilet. Fred bent over and grabbed the commode, setting it to the side. He did the same with each of our porter's loads as one by one they joined us for a brief rest on the ledge.

The porters laughed when they heard Josh give the *Poa*! response in reply to their *Mambo*!

"*Poa kichisi*!" Benjamin said back to him.

We asked Fred for a translation.

"Cool like a banana!" he said. "It means, it means..." He paused, perplexed, trying to figure out how to translate the untranslatable.

"Oh, I get it, Fred," said Josh. "It's like we say in English, 'Happy as a clam,' or 'cool beans!' "

"Cool beans?" said Fred, starting to laugh. "And then you can add more to it, you can say *Poa kichisi, kama ndisi*! 'Cool like a...like a...crazy banana!' "

This greeting became our new meme for the rest of the trek. The passing porters would guffaw whenever they heard Josh or me repeat it.

Fred grinned and chatted with the porters as they caught their breath on the ledge. Then he helped them load up again and sent them on ahead of us. He seemed much more like a comrade than a boss, and I appreciated his egalitarian style.

As we reached the top of Barranco Wall, Kilimanjaro's southern glacier slammed us in the face. The sun glinted from the brilliant mass, a hard white light that hurt the eyes. The mountain filled the sky, too big, too close to comprehend. I felt disoriented, as if hit with a weird kind of vertigo. Not dizziness from looking down, but from looking straight up at that wall of glaring ice. Standing on the mountain's neck, I knew with my rational mind that the glacier was still at least two kilometers away, more than a mile. But it seemed poised just above our heads, so close I felt I could reach out and touch one of its long white toes.

I recalled reading that the first mountaineers on Kilimanjaro were turned back by massive ice sheets so thick they covered Kibo's cone down to 4,000 meters, which was about our present elevation. The men who first summited, Hans Meyers and Ludwig Purtswcheller, spent days cutting ice steps in a 100-foot ice wall of that blocked the way to the top. Though these glaciers still looked crushingly majestic, I realized I was in the last generation that would ever see them.

The previous night I had pulled out the article Mike gave me on the most recent research of Kilimanjaro's glaciers, published in the science journal *Nature* in September 2009. It was written by a team of scientists from the University of Ohio and University of Massachusetts who have spent over a decade on Kilimanjaro measuring the exact dimensions of the ice fields, and calculating their rate of shrinkage over time. It amazed me that these remote ice fields were subject of so much scientific study. The one paragraph abstract at the start of the article shocked me:

The dramatic loss of Kilimanjaro's ice cover has attracted global attention. The three remaining ice fields on the plateau and the slopes are both shrinking laterally and rapidly thinning. Summit ice cover (areal extent) decreased ≈1% per year from 1912 to 1953 and ≈2.5% per year from 1989 to 2007. Of the ice cover present in 1912, 85% has disappeared and 26% of that present in 2000 is now gone. From 2000 to 2007 thinning (surface lowering) at the summits of the Northern and Southern Ice Fields was ≈1.9 and ≈5.1 m, respectively, which based on ice thicknesses at the summit drill sites in 2000 represents a thinning of ≈3.6% and ≈24%, respectively. Furtwängler Glacier thinned ≈50% at the drill site between 2000 and 2009. Ice volume changes (2000–2007) calculated for two ice fields reveal that nearly equivalent ice volumes are now being lost to thinning and lateral shrinking. The relative importance of different climatological drivers remains an area of active inquiry, yet several points bear consideration. Kilimanjaro's ice loss is contemporaneous with widespread glacier retreat in mid to low latitudes. The Northern Ice Field has persisted at least 11,700 years and survived a widespread drought ≈4,200 years ago that lasted ≈300 years. We present additional evidence that the combination of processes driving the current shrinking and thinning of Kilimanjaro's ice fields is unique within an 11,700-year perspective. If current climatological conditions are sustained, the ice fields atop Kilimanjaro and on its flanks will likely disappear within several decades. (from *Nature Magazine*, September 2009).

The authors were so precise in terms of measurement and so opaque about the "importance of different climatological drivers." Sure, this was written for a science journal. But it was the same problem I encountered everywhere when working with technical experts. They had buried the meaning of their work beneath a mound of data. Why couldn't they just say in plain English what they found?

They had discovered that the rate of shrinkage of Kilimanjaro's glaciers more than doubled in the past half century: from one percent per year between 1912-1953 to 2.5 percent per year between 1989-2007. The researchers also learned something new from drilling core samples all the way to the bottom of the ice. These cores, some of them 50 meters long, revealed huge amounts of information about the climate of East Africa. Like the tree rings on a giant redwood, one could count the layers of ice laid down year after year, like pages of a 11,700 year-long calendar. This was the history of the continent frozen in ice. For example, a 300-year-long drought was marked by a 30 cm layer of dust in the cores. Tiny air bubbles trapped at various depths in the ice could be analyzed to reveal the levels of carbon dioxide in the atmosphere at specific moments in time. Given how little data there was about Africa's climate in ancient times, the cores from Kilimanjaro's glaciers were something akin to unearthing the climatological Dead Sea Scrolls. But this unique record is being rapidly destroyed as the glaciers shrink, literally erasing 11,700 years of information. In just a few decades, this record will be gone. Because of this threat, the scientists decided to drill and remove additional ice cores to be stored in freezers for future generations of researchers to analyze with more sophisticated methods.

The most alarming thing that they discovered was that the top 60 years of ice is missing from the record. In the past few decades, instead of adding new layers, the surface of the glaciers has started to melt from the top down. At high altitudes such as Kilimanjaro's summit, the temperature stays below freezing, so glaciers typically don't melt to water. Instead, the intense rays of the sun turn surface ice directly into vapor. The ice gradually evaporates in a process called sublimation. But these most recent cores showed that the top 65 centimeters of the glaciers had turned to water and then refroze. Elongated bubbles and tiny channels in the ice provided certain evidence of melting in modern times – a phenomenon not found anywhere else in the glaciers' 11,700 year history.

Furtwängler Glacier, on the plateau inside the cone of Kibo, was actually discovered to be waterlogged and shrinking at a rate of five percent a year. The scientists measured its decrease at fifty percent over the past decade alone. It recently split in half, increasing the area exposed to the sun and further hastening its inevitable demise over the next several years.

"Hence, the climatological conditions currently driving the loss of Kilimanjaro's ice fields are clearly unique within an 11,700-year perspective," the researchers concluded in the *Nature* article.

I explained to Josh what I had read about the glaciers.

"You are looking at an endangered species," I said.

He looked up silently, taking in my somber words.

"It's sad," he said.

"How do you and I even begin to absorb what this means, Josh?" I said. "I think of the thousands of people who walk up to these glaciers as we are doing, they take a picture, a snapshot. This single moment, it's enough to capture the grandeur. But we don't see the time lapse photography, how over decades the glaciers are disintegrating. Like I said earlier, our human brains are good at solving human sized problems. If we had the perspective of a glacier, perhaps we would see the climate changing at a pace the planet has never experienced before."

We both looked up at the glaciers in silence.

"I am looking forward to the snowball fights, though," Josh said.

From the top of Barranco Wall the trail ran parallel to the mountain. We were in fact walking one third of the way around its circumference, from the Lava Tower on the west slope to Barafu Camp on the south east, which was where the route to the summit began. The path rose and fell across various ridges and valleys, like the wrinkles around the volcano's neck. We were growing more accustomed to the altitude now, and on level ground it was again possible to talk and walk at the same time.

"Josh, talking about how to make sense of Climate Change brings me to the next part of meme theory I wanted to discuss. This is actually where as a communications specialist, I get really interested. I think there's a special class of memes that are themselves vehicles for conveying other memes. These are communication memeplexes. Actually, nowhere in the books I've read have I come across a specific discussion about this kind of meme, or even a name for them as a class, but to me it just seems obvious..."

"You mean things like Internet, TV, books, movies, radio, newspapers, iTunes?

"Yes, exactly. These are meme systems that evolved specifically to help spread other memes."

"How about calling them 'Commplexes?'"

"Hey, I like that," I laughed. "Commplexes would include all the things we would call 'media.' There was a famous Canadian thinker from the 1960s, Marshall McLuhan, who said 'the media is the message.' His point was that our brains seem wired to enjoy connectivity. We want to watch TV, listen to the radio, read the paper, surf the Web. The information being transmitted seems almost secondary to the process. For tribal animals like us, communicating is an urge as powerful as sex and food. Modern media is really just the latest form of this need to connect that is the glue of humankind. There are many older forms of complexes..."

"Like writing, theater, music, art, dance, storytelling," Josh rattled them off.

"Yes, these all go back, oh, who knows how long? I remember seeing a vase from Serbia that was 6,500 years old that depicted a woman wearing a mask and dancing. So there was some element of performance and storytelling going on. And *Gilgamesh*, the world's earliest epic, is thought to be over 4,000 years old. Storytelling, I think, is absolutely key to our identity as humans. There's something in us that just loves a story. I think since humans first sat around in the evening, they told each other about the events of the day. 'Oh, let me tell you how I escaped a saber-toothed tiger!' And we are all the wiser for hearing the tale. When someone says, 'Let me tell you a story,' that opens our ears. So we have Bible stories and news stories, histories, mysteries, children's stories–"

"And the stories we used to make up in the car?"

When Josh was young, the two of us used to tell stories back and forth while I drove him to and from school. He would voice the main character in all of these adventures, a spunky trickster called "the Little Mouse" who carried a magic back pack filled with whatever he needed to solve problems and get out of scrapes. I would voice the character of 'Josh' as well as other supporting voices. Through a magic door in Josh's bedroom, the two friends could travel to any place, any time, and any imaginary realm. Together Josh and the Little Mouse riffed on every fable, myth, and Disney movie we could think of, from *The Labors of Heracles* to *The Lion King*.

"Yes," I nodded, "telling these stories created a hundred worlds we shared. They are some of my best memories with you growing up. In the same way, I believe storytelling connects us all profoundly as human beings."

We moved to the side of the trail to let a group of porters pass.

"*Mambo?*" they called out to us.

"*Poa kichisi, kama ndisi!*" Josh called back and they laughed.

"So here's what I learned only recently about stories that fascinates me," I said as we resumed walking. "The brain actually recalls narrative stories differently than it recalls facts about the world. Objective facts–information, concepts, the rough-guide principles we talked about earlier–these memes are stored in the left hemisphere of the brain. You remember right-brain/left brain theory?"

"Sure. We studied it in my high school psych class. The two hemispheres of the brain have different functions. The left is the linear thinking, conceptual, language processing part of the brain, and the right is emotional, spatial, non-verbal, intuitive, and creative."

"Right. Now, according to the most recent brain research, facts pertaining to our understanding of the world are basically stored and recalled in the left hemisphere. But stories about our life are stored and recalled in the right hemisphere."

"No, that can't be. The right is non-verbal. It doesn't store language..."

"That's what I thought, Josh. I couldn't make sense of it at first. Here's what I learned: The right hemisphere is the one which processes the incoming sensations from our body. There are huge webs of neurons clustered in parts of our body such as our heart, our intestines. The feeling from these webs travel up the spinal cord and get processed in the emotional centers of the brain, and then into the right hemisphere. These sensations provide us with a kind of intuition and inner knowing. So we talk about our gut instinct, our heartache–"

"Dad, this is exactly what we deal with in massage," Josh broke in. "In training I learned how massage often releases deep emotions and trauma that may be locked in the body."

"Right, this fits exactly. The brain's right hemisphere basically mediates between the body's felt experience, including emotions, and the logical and verbal left hemisphere that tries to make sense of it all. So, what happens when we tell a story about ourselves? If I just state biographical facts–I was born August 8, 1958 in Toronto. I attended Balmy Beach Public School– it's boring. It's not a story at all. When you tell a story, your brain floods with remembered images, sounds and body sensations. Your whole body responds as you talk as if you are reliving the event. You tense up with recalled anger, tear up with sadness, or flush with embarrassment."

"And this is a big part of acting," Josh jumped in again, "putting yourself into the emotional state of your character."

"Absolutely. So when we tell our own story, we reactivate the emotional states in our mind and in our body that we experienced at the time the story took place. Let me demonstrate. Let me think about a childhood memory. Okay, getting in a fight at school with a bully. I get the memory as a flood of sensations. I see his freckled face in a sneer, his angry blue eyes focused on me. I hear the other kids yelling, goading us on, closing in a circle around us. I feel him punching my stomach, my mouth. His fists are so fast I just see a blur. I taste blood on my lip and feel my face going numb. A kick to my crotch, and I'm contracting in pain and in shame, falling down to my knees and curling into a ball. There's no more time, it's like it's happening now. My right brain is activating all these stored feelings and images. I experience it like an inner movie. My left brain is rushing to put into words all these sensations, like a sports commentator's play by play of a game. But here's what happens now. As I am telling my story to you, your left brain decodes the words of my narrative, and then they explode into pictures and sensations that play out on the screen of your mind. You are making your own version of my movie. As your right brain processes this flood of sensations, you feel it inside your own body. Maybe it's not exactly what I feel, but close enough that we are in a sense sharing the experience. You might wince when I wince. You might burn with my shame. It's a miraculous transmission when you think about it. My stories can literally live in you, and your stories can live in me."

"Dad–that's terrible though."

I had blown through my story, genuinely reliving it while I spoke, but then moving on with my train of thought. I had not stopped to consider the impact on Josh as he walked behind me. I felt a bit embarrassed now for what I had said.

"Ah, it's just an example. When I was a kid, I won some fights and lost some fights. I remember another time, getting this kid in a headlock, and hanging on like he was some kind of bull I was riding, so afraid he would bust loose and kill me. His friends were around me, shouting, 'Bite him Percy, bite him!' I held on until he surrendered. You, though, I only remember you getting into a fight once in school."

"Yeah, in first grade. I got sent to the office."

"I recall you telling me about it. It was the first week of school, and this kid came up to you…"

"And he said to me, 'I bet you can't hit me,' so I hit him and knocked him down. We both got sent to the office."

"You know, that probably stopped anybody else from bullying you at that school. Do you remember ever having trouble like that?"

Josh shrugged. "I don't think so."

"I remember Chris when you were in grade three, I would see him chasing you. I was really concerned. You told me he was your friend. You said you were just playing a game. But I could tell from the look in his eye he was out for trouble."

"Yeah, he used to chase me and I'd run away. I remember thinking it was a great game. Every now and then he would catch me and sit on me, and I would squeak when he bounced up and down. I thought it was hilarious."

"I remember you telling me about this. I realized this poor kid was trying to bully you, but you just didn't get it. To you it was all a big joke."

"Yeah, and Chris turned into the sweetest guy in high school. We became good friends."

We walked in silence for a while, breathing hard, crunching over fragments of shale. We had been walking along a stretch of the trail that meandered back and forth across the south side of the mountain. The land was a dull grey wasteland, littered with broken fragments of rock. The tendons on the back of my knees legs were still aching, but other than that I was pleased to feel my body responding well to the rigors of the trek. Walking had become my natural rhythm. Even when tired, movement felt better than rest. Fred pointed out a faraway hill, Karanga Camp, and said it was our destination for the night.

"You know," said Josh, "if I were on campus and someone pointed to a place that far away and told me we have to walk to it, I would be like, 'Oh man, it's too far!' But here, it's like, 'Oh boy, there's our camp, just a thousand miles away! Let's get moving!'"

We shouldered our packs and pushed on.

"Josh, this talk about stories is really clarifying something for me. I think the use of story is what makes myths so powerful. Myth helps organizes our belief systems into a coherent narrative, whether it's Thor creating thunder when he strikes his hammer or Adam and Eve eating the apple and being cast out of Eden.

"You know, I also studied this in acting somewhere. It's like we're covering the same ground but in way different ways.

"Maybe you're thinking of Aristotle's *Poetics*. His definition of plot is mythos. It means 'story,' but it's a special kind of story, the story that tells–no, reminds–people about what their beliefs and values are. You see, ancient people didn't really have history. They had dramas and epics and sagas that turned their shared memories of legends and rituals into stories. What's new for me is realizing that like a story, myth gets processed in our right brain and connects to the nerves of our body. Through stories we literally integrate this sense of mythos into the fiber of our being, like a tree with deep roots. In contrast, when the facts of science are communicated as objective facts, they don't have the same kind of resonance. That's why when information is processed only in the left hemisphere, it doesn't stick as well.

"I think this is why the memes of science are so easily rejected by Fundamentalists. I think the mythos of Christianity, the story of Jesus dying for our sins, is what makes this particular religion so appealing. I gave my heart to Jesus in my late teens because it gave my life this dramatic but coherent narrative. It connected me personally to God. Jesus died on the cross for *my* sins. That was 'the greatest story ever told.' True or not, it's a powerful narrative. I remember last spring I saw a YouTube video of a Republican member of Congress who testified that he did not believe in Climate Change. He then explained why. He said that after the great flood described in the book of Genesis, God promised Noah he would never bring about such a catastrophic change in the weather again. Therefore no Climate Change. How could any scientist possibly produce enough climate data points to convince this congressman to change his mind?"

"Wow," said Josh, shaking his head.

"The mythos might be false, but if the story evokes a strong gut feeling, a congruence deep in our body, then we will believe it as if it's a capital-T Truth. And if the facts that don't fit with the mythos, it's the facts that will be rejected."

"So, the problem with Climate Change is that it doesn't make a good story?"

"Yes, I think that's it. I mean, the narrative for Climate Change is pretty clear. The earth's atmosphere is like a greenhouse. By producing too many greenhouse gases, humans are raising the planet's temperature. Too much of an increase, and the global climate changes, creating floods and hurricanes and droughts, rising sea levels, killing off millions of species that can't adapt, creating famine and plague, and war and death."

"So, it's just a *lousy* story," said Josh. "It's flat, like when you were telling 'just the facts' of your childhood. There's not a mythos. I mean, I guess there could be one. But it's not personal. At the same time, it's scary. Who would want to believe in Climate Change if there was any way you could avoid it?"

"I think you've nailed the problem," I sighed. "It's hard for any person to connect this impending global catastrophe to their individual life. There's no obvious way to make a significant difference. The option of totally changing our economy, stop using coal and oil, it just seems too hard. It's also too wrenching for our minds to believe that the good life we have been living could be the cause of our destruction. Our cars, our factories, our furnaces–these are suddenly bad things? It doesn't fit the mythos so many of us have about The American Dream: progress, growth, capitalism. I think if there were a giant meteorite headed our way that was going to destroy the earth, every country would pool its resources and spend trillions of dollars to build a giant spaceship and go blow it up. That would be a narrative we could believe in. Or if Climate Change were caused by terrorists, Communists, Nazis, or the Devil, we could get behind the story of defeating an evil enemy. But scientific analysis says the enemy is *us*. That's a tough mythos to sell."

"It's like you were saying earlier about Kilimanjaro," said Josh. "There's a story in the ice. But the experts who can read it can't tell it like a story. So it's easy not to hear it."

I shook my head grimly.

"You know, the very strength of science is that it keeps us from the errors of mythos, from getting committed to a set of memes that we adopt because of congruence with what we think we know. Science demands skepticism. It enshrines the idea that the 'rough guide,' small t-truth is the best we've ever got, so we must constantly and rigorously evaluate our memes and reject the ones that can't stand up to scrutiny. If only we could enshrine that principle in the story of, say, a son of god with an electron microscope or prophet with a spectrometer, then we'd have a religion I could get behind! Instead, science has heroes like Pasteur, Darwin and Einstein who turned out to be right some of the time and wrong some of the time–which is exactly what you should expect from a scientist. But as a result, science has a tough time competing against the memes of religion, and even astrology, for a place in our heads."

It was just past noon as we climbed the hilltop of Karanga. Though it was still early in the day, close to a hundred tents already speckled the broad barren slope with patches of blue, yellow and green. As we marched into camp, I noticed the rangers weighing bags of trash. I remembered Fred telling me at the start of the trek that the rangers were strict about tracking garbage, so that everything packed in was indeed packed out. It was good to see that they were really doing it. When I stopped to think about it, there was surprisingly little litter along the trail, and the campsites looked remarkably clean.

The mountain dominated the sky to the north of us. To the south, the volcanic plateau fell off into a distant sea of clouds, now so far below that it was difficult to remember there was another world down there, farms and villages and a city submerged beneath the grey waves. Land around the camp seemed lifeless except for a few rough sprouts of coarse grass here and there. A dozen white-necked ravens flitted about–greater numbers than I had yet seen in any one place. They hopped between the tents. Fred had warned us told not to leave anything shiny on the ground. These opportunistic thieves nabbed any watches and sunglasses left unattended. I imagined the birds back at their nests, hanging out like gangsters in their classy shades and Rolexes.

We were not used to ending our day's trek before lunch. The free afternoon felt like a holiday from our vacation. I kicked off my boots and put on some tennis shoes. Sully brought us warm water to wash our hands and faces, and then welcomed us to lunch. The dinner tent was already up and ready for us. Yet again our inventive cook had prepared a surprise. This time it was a meal that was so close to home, we didn't even realize at first there was Tanzanian twist: fried chicken and french fries. But in with the french fries we found some peculiar, squishy, reddish brown things: slices of deep fried banana.

I munched a bit of banana. It tasted gummy, kind of mealy, with just a hint of sweetness.

"I want to talk a bit more about stories," I said to Josh, chewing a banana, "and one more kind of memeplex that helps us create a sense of our place in the world."

"Sure," Josh said through a mouthful of chicken.

"The books I've read about memes talk about one memeplex which integrates all the other meme systems together, that binds them and creates a unified sense of cohesion in our minds."

"You mean, one meme to rule them all?"

"Yes, precisely! I'm talking about the memeplex of the self, which memeticists call the selfplex. Our sense of personal identity draws our memories, beliefs, stories, and all the other memes together and organizes them into a congruent whole. It makes all the memes in our mind seem like 'mine.' "

Josh stopped chewing.

"So you are saying my *self* is just a meme? Your *self* is just a meme?"

"Not exactly. I am saying that our brains organize our other memes around the concept of 'self' and that this *concept* is a meme."

"Dad, I don't think people are going to like the idea that all they are is a meme."

"You're right. It's much less satisfying than the story of God breathing his spirit into clay and making the first humans, or that we are reincarnated souls. We want to have a story that makes our self into something solid, like a rock. Anything less and it feels like we are explaining the self away.

"It's funny when you think about it," I continued. "Our sense of self is at the very center of our being. Yet scientists and philosophers struggle to explain it, and mystics can only use metaphors. In the West, we glorify the self, nurture our sense of self esteem, raise our consciousness, pursue our individual right to happiness. In the East, however, the individual self is seen as a disruptive force that must be sublimated to society. In Buddhism, the self is seen as an illusion that causes suffering. The Buddhist Sutras say: 'Happy are the enlightened ones: for them the thought "I am" ceases to arise.'

"I remember one day when I was writing one of my books on Buddhism, it hit me that I should teach you about the illusion of self. You were about six. You were playing with your Megazords on the kitchen floor. I was sitting at the kitchen table reading. So I said to you:

" 'You know, you are not really Josh.'

" 'What do you mean?' you said to me in a panicky voice.

" 'I mean, "Josh" is the name that we use. But it's not really you.'

" 'Who, who am I?' you said, starting to cry. You were starting to freak out. Your voice got all high and quivery.

" 'It's okay, it's okay, you are Josh, you are Josh,' I backpedalled. Then we played a game or something to help you forget about it."

"Jeez. Dad, what were you thinking?"

"Well, by then I was realizing that precipitating a metaphysical crisis in a six year old was not good parenting technique after all."

Josh laughed.

"You want the last of my banana fries?"

He shook his head. I poured us both some tea and continued.

"Unfortunately, as Buddhists will admit, getting to enlightenment is extremely rare and difficult. The meme of self is very tenacious. Many Eastern-style spiritual teachings actually speak about the self as a destructive and negative force. But that made it seem like a real thing. How could something that is an illusion be so powerful, I wondered? Meme theory and the idea of the selfplex explained this seeming paradox. Suddenly it made perfect sense to me. It's the stories we tell about who we are that create the memeplex of our self. Those memes don't exist like a thing, like a rock. So the self is in a sense an illusion we attach to our physical being. On the one hand it gives us a sense of personal identity that helps us organize our existence. It provides a sense of congruence for our being. On the other hand, it can make us rigid, stuck, and resistant to change.

"I realized Buddhism was wrong on this important point. It's not belief in the self that makes us suffer. It's our belief in our stories about our self that makes us suffer. When we commit to these stories we make ourselves into something solid and inflexible. Our selfplex is constructed of stories, anecdote by anecdote, as if brick by brick. These stories have a useful social and personal function. But like bricks, our stories of ourselves can easily get built into walls as solid as any prison. We say, 'That's just who I am,' and we get stuck. But if we keep in the back of our mind that our stories are a personal mythos–a narrative that helps us live coherent lives in a small-t truth, rough guide kind of way–then our sense of self can stay flexible. We can keep growing and changing in response to new experiences."

"This reminds me of that movie we saw together," said Josh, "*I Heart Huckabees*."

"The one with Dustin Hoffman and Lilly Tomlin as the existential detectives?"

"Yeah. I'm thinking of the part where Jude Law's character, Brad, is telling everybody the story about how he outsmarted Shania Twain, who is a celebrity spokesperson for his company. He says Shania hates mayo and she can't eat chicken salad. But one time that was all they had on the set to eat, so he told her it was tuna. She's suspicious–"

"I remember," I jumped in. "He tells her he's allergic to mayo himself, and eats two sandwiches to prove to her there's none in it. But of course he's lying. He says she eats one and a half sandwiches before she realizes she's eating chicken salad and liking it."

"Right," Josh jumped back in. "So Brad tells this story to make him look really cool. He's outsmarting this big, fussy celebrity in this funny way. Everybody laughs. The detectives confront him about it. They ask, why does he tell this same story all the time? Brad denies it. So they play back the mini tape recorder they have been using to record his conversations and he hears himself telling the tuna fish story over and over, using exactly the same words. You see Brad's face as he listens. First he looks annoyed, then horrified, then crushed. He realizes for the first time how pathetic he is, how this story is a huge prop. Like everything else in his life, his house, his cute girlfriend, his job. It's all just props.

And they he goes off to this meeting where he's going to be promoted. The bosses ask him to tell the tuna fish story. He starts to gag on his own words, and vomits in his hand."

"So," I said, "just like Brad in the movie, each of us selects a set of stories we use to construct our sense of self. We put some things in, leave other things out. We simplify, we edit. We tend to portray our self as the hero in the narrative of our lives. But the stories we tell create a crust of self that is hollow in the center. I remember one thing about my own crust when I was a teenager. As you know, I was a super Type-A overachiever in high school. I used to rake in all these academic and sports awards. My dresser was packed with trophies and medals and certificates and things like that that I put out on display."

"Kind of like you were saying, 'See, I did it!' Having something to show for what you did?"

"Exactly. But you know, that was never the whole story."

I took a deep breath. My heart was racing suddenly, and my mouth went dry. Why was it hard to talk with Josh about this? I continued:

"When I was a little kid, my dad used to call me a 'clot,' a word he made up that meant stupid and clumsy. He would say it whenever he was mad at me for doing something dumb. I was just a kid. Of course I didn't know how to do things the right way and made mistakes. He used to make me feel so stupid and ashamed. I remember one time we were walking on the beach, and he started writing 'Tim is a clot' in the sand, in huge letters, over and over. I followed behind, trying to rub it out, crying while he laughed. So when I look back, I have to wonder if that was part of why I needed to get the best marks at everything in school, to erase those words. When I got an award, I could say to myself: 'See you are not a clot,' and feel some relief, some security in that grade or that trophy. Those were the bricks in my walls, the story of my success. The point is, when we try to leave the unpleasant details out of the story, when they remain untold, they get bricked in unconsciously, creating a dark side, a shadow. So for me, sure, I became a star student. But I lived with this unconscious fear that at any moment I would be exposed as a fraud. I could never be good enough to really relax. I always had to be the best. I was driven."

"Dad, that's really fucked up. I can't believe Skipper would ever do that to you. He loves you."

"My dad had his own childhood issues, Josh. He loved me, but sometimes he tormented me," I shrugged.

We sat in silence for a moment.

"You know, this is really good, the tea," said Josh, sipping. We were on our third cup. "And lunch was tasty. But where's dessert?"

"Welcome fruit pudding!"

Sully deposited our dessert, and flashed a smile on the way out.

"I love Sully," said Josh. "You know earlier today he saw me looking at the camera, and he said, 'Photo? Photo!' So I said I would take his picture. He got a chair and posed. He wanted to see it. Then we chatted about soccer for ten minutes. Even though I hardly understood a sentence of what he said, it was great. I love his intensity. When I was feeling bad, he would say to me, 'You finish that tea, then I get you more. Then you feel better!' "

"He's really taking care of you."

"Yeah. Definitely the best waiter I ever had. When we got here today, I just gave him a big hug. I was so happy to see him. I love the feeling around here, you know, being called 'brother' and 'friend.' So much compassion. They are our guide and our waiter, but I feel so close to them."

"I appreciate Fred, too. He's been so concerned for you. He really thinks things through in advance for both of us."

"Oh, while you were talking, I remember I want to say something about the crust thing," said Josh. "Especially in this Facebook age, and Twitter and whatever, people just love telling other people what they're up to. I mean, me too. There's just a satisfaction in saying 'Well, I'm off to Kilimanjaro!' It's great to be able to tell people about it. But sometimes I read people's posts and I get the feeling that they're doing it so that they can tell us about it. Especially with charity work or an internship or something, they just post all over, and it's all about them doing this thing. I kind of wonder: 'When do you have time to do the thing you're spending so much time telling us about you doing, really making it clear that you're doing it?' Sometimes it seems like they're doing less for the charity or even for themselves, and more to create a good impression on their friends, using Facebook to create a deliberate perception in us of who they want to be."

I nodded, taking this in.

"You want to switch to Milo, Josh? I'll make you a cup."

"Sure, thanks," said Josh, "I'm thinking this is probably what makes it so hard to hear something other than what you perceive yourself to be. If someone says, 'You're selfish', you go 'Woah! Hold on! No I'm not! That's not how I defined myself, what's your problem buddy?' "

"Right, Gossip, slander, Ye–"

"Dad, that's the sugar bowl. You are putting Milo in the sugar bowl, not my cup."

I looked down at my spoon. Indeed I was. I laughed.

"So it makes sense," Josh continued, "why people get really defensive when somebody points out that they are not what they think they are. You know, Mom sometimes floors me with this. I came home at the end of term a month ago, and she starts yelling at me, 'You've got to learn to be more independent!' It felt like such a personal attack. I felt like I spent the whole year becoming independent, living on my own. Even the year before, with massage school, I felt really independent. It was a big thing I defined for myself, this independence. I felt like, Hello? Mom? Do I need to pull out my trophies to show you who I am?"

I laughed. We sipped our sweet, chocolaty Milo.

"You know, Josh, when I was telling you that story about my dad calling me a clot, I started wondering–do you have any stories like that about me?"

Josh paused for a beat. "Well, there was that rooster I was so frickin' terrified of when I was three and we lived on the farm. To me, it was always hunting me down, so I just stayed clear of it. But you took it upon yourself to help me conquer this fear. I remember one day you picked me up, carried me over to the coop, and set me down with the rooster just a few feet away. You said, 'All right now, walk towards him, give him a big old fuzzy hug! Yeah, get in his striking range. Go Josh, go!' "

"That's not what I said!"

"But that was your attitude. I remember staring in utter horror at this thing that was just as tall as me. When I think about it now, it's still pretty scary. I remember going towards it, taking really tiny, tiny steps, my eyes tearing up and thinking, my dad's trying to kill me! He's going to make the rooster eat me! And you yelling at me, 'Come on Josh, you can do it!' It was a blinding blur of feathers after that. I remember it rushing forward and either it clawed me or pecked me on the face I think."

"Not on the face," I interrupted.

"Maybe it was the hand. Maybe you were trying to get me to feed him. It pecked me somewhere. I was bleeding. You picked me up and you were like, 'Argh! Oh, Jeez, I'm sorry! What have I done?!' You carried me into the house to put on a bandage. It hurt a lot, which just amplified my terror."

"I remember this all, Josh. Oh man, I felt horrible. I was so stupid. I'm so sorry. What did you think when it was over?"

"Well, you know, Dad, I really didn't comprehend at all. I felt that somehow you were going to teach me something through this strange ritual. But I really didn't have a clue what it was."

Fred ducked into the tent. He frowned at us, like a scolding parent.

"Get lots of rest this afternoon," he said. "Tomorrow night you will not sleep."

Shivering, standing at the side of the pool in swim class, I covered my flabby tummy with my folded arms. The girls giggled. Were they laughing at me? I was twelve and I was fat. When I looked in the mirror I felt disgust. That summer I went on a diet. I lost seventeen pounds.

"I knew that was the moment you started to become a man," my father tells me, "when you took your life into your own hands."

To me it was a moment born in shame. I was just trying to escape being someone I loathed.

"For me, that moment happened when I was thirteen," my dad continued. "My father had been killed in the war, and my mother sent me to live on a farm while she fell apart in Toronto. I was told the farmer would pay me ten dollars a month for my work plus room and board. The day I arrived he gave me a shovel and told me to clean the manure out of the barn. I worked on that barn for three days. Then when I finished, the farmer told me I could start shoveling out the outhouse. I told him I wasn't shoveling shit any more. He said, 'Oh yes you are.' I said, 'Then I quit and I want to be paid my wages. You owe me a dollar' He said, 'You can take a chicken as your wages, but you have to catch and kill it yourself.' He laughed at me. Next day I plucked the feathers off that chicken, sitting on the rear of a truck, hitchhiking back to Toronto."

Chapter Six

In the Blue Tent

Karanga Camp

After lunch Josh and I escaped the intense solar radiation in the shelter of our tent. Until that point in our journey, we had spent almost all of our daylight hours on Kilimanjaro walking. So it was quite enjoyable just to lounge on top of our sleeping bags with nowhere to go and nothing to do. Sunlight filtered through the nylon fabric, turning it a soothing shade of swimming-pool blue. We opened the flaps at the front and back so that a gentle breeze flowed through.

"You know, Josh, talking with you about my dad earlier, and how understanding his story helped me make better sense of my own life, I realized I've never really told you my story. Some amusing tales, sure. But not the real story, the pieces I have put together to create my own selfplex. I thought, maybe you'd like to hear it?"

Josh turned to his side on his sleeping bag to face me. He propped his head up on one arm and looked at me with an open, expectant expression. It reminded me of all the times when he was a boy that I had sat on the side of his bed, about to open a new chapter of some book we were reading.

"So tell me the story, Dad."

"Okay, but I'd like to start by telling you what I hate about family stories. As an adult I used to find it hard to tolerate going home and having Mom and Dad tell the same funny anecdotes over and over again. I felt they were always painting this picture of our 'Perfect Happy Family,' as I called it. I didn't like it because

I knew it wasn't the whole truth. I was there. I lived the painful stuff too. It's as if my parents took the nice and cute fragments from our family life and put them together into a beautiful mosaic that they want to remember. But the other stuff's buried in the grout between the shiny fragments, that's also part of the story. Even if I don't consciously remember everything, the other stuff is in me too. So the grout is want I want to include, when I tell my own story to you."

Science Geek

"When I was in high school, I was a math and science whiz. I saw myself as being a very smart person, and because of that, being exceptional. I developed this strong Type-A personality. But I was really locked in my head. My friends used to tease me when playing hockey because I would never just shoot the puck by instinct. I had to pause and think about the angle. 'Figure it out mathematically, Tim!' my teammates would yell. When it came to relationships, I often quipped that I wanted to be a scientist because 'chemical reactions are much easier to predict than human reactions.' My young crust of self was obsessed with being the best. I won the trophy for best all-around student accomplishments every year during high school."

"So this is why you were so frustrated with me in school?" Josh burst in.

"Josh, I would look at your assignment transcripts and see 'A, A, B, A, D, D, E,' and go 'Arghhhhh! He could ace this course so easily, what is he doing?' "

"Well," said Josh, "I didn't exactly turn to math and science for the meaning of my life. In fact, I sort of preferred the randomness of human reactions to the stupid predictability of chemical reactions. I got kind of bored with them. But go on."

"The part of the story I never told you is that when I would walk to and from school, I would curse myself. 'You bastard, you piece of crap,' stuff like that. My sister, who slept in the room across the hall, told me I would sometimes scream obscenities at myself in my sleep, waking her up. Where was that coming from? Just today, talking about my dad humiliating me as a little kid, it hit me that perhaps that's where it started, this god-like figure calling me a clot. By the time I was a teen, it was my own voice inside my own head yelling that I was crap. So, my life was excellence and trophies on the surface. But with this weird self-hating going on underneath.

Born Again Christian

"The summer I turned 18, I went to Saskatchewan to work as a pipeline surveyor. The crews slept in public campgrounds. I used to walk out alone onto the prairie in the evenings and look up at these incredible stars and Milky Way, like the sky here on Kilimanjaro. I felt this kind of bliss that was different than anything else I had known. I felt connected to God. Around that time I was partnered up with a guy named Bob who was a Bible college student. Bob and I discussed theology all day as we drove along the lines. Had I given my life to Christ, Bob wanted to know? Not really. I loved God, sure, but I didn't like the idea that to be committed to Christ I would have to give up sex until marriage, as the Bible clearly said. I was really horny as a teenager. It had taken me until my junior year of high school to find a girlfriend who would have sex with me, and I was not about to give that up.

"A few days later I met a fifteen year old girl whose family was staying at the campground. She thought she was pregnant and that her father was going to kick her out of the house because of it. She was near suicidal. I was able to talk with her and pray with her. And guess what? She had her period the next day. I felt my prayers were answered. I also felt God was sending me a sign that my life could be about more than solving equations and selfishly seeking sex. If I surrendered to Him, I could become a healing force in people's lives. Maybe this was a real way to become good, not through good grades, but through doing good in God's eyes? And if the price God demanded for this new life was giving up sex, well, I could do it. So my story changed. I stayed celibate for the next four years of my life, from age 18 to 22.

"Giving up sex was definitely the hardest thing about being a Born-again Christian. I remember attending a Pentecostal revival meeting during which the pastor said Jesus was going to return for the Rapture in three to five years, and that we young people should dedicate ourselves to God's work and stay celibate until He returned. I recall praying. 'Okay, Lord, three-to-five years I can handle. But please don't take any longer because I don't think I could make it...' "

"Dad, I'm really struggling here to find something in common with you. It seems everything you were, I'm not. I was never a religious type. I never strived to be the straight-A student. I just wanted to get through school and have fun. I don't think I ever cursed myself. Then having a relationship just for sex? I would never...I didn't need Christianity to tell me. I had my own guiding compass for that. Sex has never been the most important thing for me. If I had to choose between sex and some greater cause I believed in–certainly not Christianity, but something else–I could do it without this sense you had that it was so unbearable. It would be, like, okay."

"I was really very serious about Christianity, very intense too," I went on. "I wanted to go to Bible college. I wanted to become a pastor or a missionary."

"No shit? Dad, this is hard to imagine."

"Yes. I was convinced this was the path for me. Then, when I went for my interview at the college they told me I would have to shave my beard. At age 19 I had a bush on my face that made me look and feel 25. 'But Jesus had a beard,' I argued with them. 'That may be,' the college officials told me, 'But you are not Jesus, and you can't have a beard here.' So I said goodbye to my dream of Bible college–"

"Are you kidding?" Josh interrupted with a laugh. "I thought you were going to say goodbye to your beard! You could give up sex, but not your beard?!"

"Well, you put it that way and it does sound crazy. But I knew if I had trouble accepting arbitrary rules over facial hair, I was probably going to have trouble with the whole Bible college package. So instead I enrolled in the study of Philosophy at the University of British Columbia. I figured this way I could go to divinity school when I graduated.

Philosophy Student

"Some of my Christian friends urged me not to study philosophy. They feared I would lose my faith. I replied, 'What's the point of a faith that you have to shield from reason?' My best friend at UBC was a hard-core Marxist Existentialist named John. He and I spent literally thousands of hours arguing over God and dialectical materialism. John turned me on to Nietzsche, whose virulently anti-Christian writings perversely attracted me. I loved his aphorism, 'That which does not kill me makes me stronger.' So I began reading Nietzsche determined to sharpen my faith against the whetstone of his atheism. To my surprise I found in Nietzsche a kindred spirit: someone hungry for reality, intolerant of lazy thinking, and ruthless with his own mind."

"Um, what do you mean?"

"He was always ready to sacrifice a cherished idea on the altar of truth.

"But you said there was no capital-T Truth..."

"Yeah, Nietzsche attacked anything that smacked of dogma. He was also highly skeptical of 'truths' gathered by experience, including science. What he advocated instead was a very specific kind of truth, the will 'not to allow ourselves to be deceived.' He was the first thinker I came across who challenged the idea that human consciousness was something that made us special.

Instead he saw consciousness as the tiniest, most superficial and common part of who we are. To him, consciousness was like the skin of the orange, the outermost layer of the mind. He wrote about the power of the unconscious before Freud was born, before there even was a science of psychology. Nietzsche opened me to the thrilling possibility that my own mind was unknown territory and that life was not a puzzle to be solved, but mystery to be explored. Some of my teachers told me that Nietzsche's desire to push boundaries was what drove him insane at age 44. I thought to myself: It's worth it! That's what I wanted, to dig beneath the skin of my orange, the skin of my culture, the skin of the world, to burrow in deep into it like a maggot, right to the core.

"I was dismayed to discover that my philosophy teachers had not even read Nietzsche. They did not consider him a philosopher, and there was not a single course on him taught in our entire department. My advisor suggested I take classes in Comparative Literature instead. It hit me then that my teachers were not interested in the kind of relentless questioning that Nietzsche had excited in me. They only wanted us to memorize and analyze the writings of the dead men they considered philosophers. They were grave keepers.

"After my second year at UBC, I took a semester off. I spent eight months hitchhiking around Europe. I wanted to see the history of my culture for myself. So I travelled through England, France, Italy, Germany, Greece, Israel, Egypt: the cradles of Western philosophy and religion. I loved roaming around all on my own. I met women along the way and fell in love with some of them. I began to realize that my vow of celibacy was actually functioning as a shield against intimacy. Did God want me to live my life running scared like this? One evening at a bar in Ireland a young woman named Mary started buying me pints of Guinness. The two of us ended up back at my tent, which was pitched in a field behind the pub. We were talking, and I was getting this strange vibe from her.

" 'What do you want, Mary?' I asked.

"In her sweet, lilting voice, she replied, 'You.'

"The sex that followed was not very good. We seemed to have a lot of trouble at first. When it was over and she kissed me goodbye and left my tent, it suddenly hit me why. Mary was a virgin."

"So Dad," Josh started laughing, "You ended your four years of celibacy for the sake of God by–"

"Yeah, don't say it…

"From Ireland to Israel I spoke with many Christians about their faith. I learned a lot about whole branches of Christianity of which I was ignorant. I saw the Vatican, Notre Dame, the Black Madonna of Czestochowa. In Jerusalem a Greek Orthodox monk at the Church of the Holy Sepulture told me his faith rested on the Holy Fire that God sent into the Sepulture each Easter Sunday. I began to see there were dozens of different Christianities. Traveling through Israel I visited all the famous places from Jesus' life, Bethlehem, Nazareth, Herod's Temple in Jerusalem. I remember looking at this large silver cross that marked the spot where Christ was crucified, according to Catholic and Orthodox believers. Seeing this place filled with incense and chanting, gold and silver everywhere, I realized it was all just tradition, just a story. Nowhere was there any actual historical evidence that Jesus died in this spot. I'm probably one of the few Christians who visited the Holy Land and found that it weakened his faith."

"I returned to finish university disillusioned with both academic philosophy and Evangelical Christianity. I decided neither to go to graduate school nor to apply for Divinity School. Instead, I wanted to travel more. I remember in my last semester I spent a lot of time walking along the shores of Wreck Beach, just below UBC campus. I looked across the water towards Asia, where half of humanity lived. It hit me that I knew nothing about this world, its people, its ancient spiritual traditions. I knew this would be the next step for me.

Buddhist Wanderer

"I worked for two years on oil rigs and seismic crews to pay off my college debts. Then I bought a small back pack and a one-way ticket to New Delhi. I spent the next two years wandering through India, Nepal, Bangladesh, Burma, Thailand, Malaysia, Indonesia, China and eventually Tibet. Though I still considered myself a Christian of some sort, I was eager to learn everything that Asia had to teach me. I stayed in Buddhist monasteries and Hindu ashrams, slept in caves in the Himalayas and in the homes of rural villagers and urban slum dwellers. I wanted to experience for myself the esoteric traditions of the oldest cultures on the planet. I also wanted to know what life was really like for the poorest of the poor. I wanted to discipline my mind with meditation, endure the suffering of others, and break out of the box of my own middle-class mind. I wanted to tear up my old map of the world and see it all with new eyes.

'It was exhilarating, freeing, and at times terrifying. Traveling alone so much of the time, I found myself doing things I never would have done at home, like having an affair with a married Thai woman in Bangkok, or trying hallucinogenic mushrooms–"

"*What*? Dad, I cannot believe you ever lectured me about illegal drugs!"

"Well, it wasn't exactly illegal in Sumatra. But I admit I was lucky that some of the riskier things I did–walking into war zones, climbing sheer cliffs alone in the Himalayas, going off with a local Indonesian tribal girl to her remote village, swimming in shark-infested waters, hitchhiking into military-occupied areas of Tibet–never got me killed. In the end it, I developed this wild, free sense that if I was alert and adaptable, I could do almost anything I wanted, and live my life whatever way I pleased.

"One of the most mind-blowing experiences took place when I was in Ladakh in the Indian Himalayas. I was studying Tibetan Buddhism in a monastery. One of the core tenets of Buddhism is that our everyday "reality" is based on the illusion that there are solid objects that persist through time, while actually nothing is permanent, everything changes. Through meditation, one can concentrate one's awareness and perceive raw sense data as the kaleidoscopic flux of the universe. So I climbed into the mountains and spent a week in a cave meditating. The Aha! moment came for me on the last day. I was meditating on water dripping at the edge of a small waterfall. Suddenly reality slowed down and I could perceive the individual drops as if I were watching single frames of a movie reel. Instead of seeing one drop fall, I saw the drop as three separate images: a sparkling dot at the top, middle and bottom of each successive frame. I realized it was my mind that stitched these images together the illusion of a falling drop. This was my first experience of seeing first-hand that everyday reality is actually constructed by the processes of the brain.

"But the strangest encounter I had at this monastery, the thing that changed me most, was a spontaneous hallucination. I was doing an extended meditation practice that monks do to break down the delusion of desire. The idea is to vividly imagine a naked woman (or whatever you feel the most sexual desire for), and then deconstruct the image into tiny bits, and watch desire disappear. So for example, perhaps I desire her long dark hair. How about a lock of it? How about a single strand of it? How about a two inch piece? Definitely I feel no desire for a two inch hair clipping. Then you build the image back up again, seeing that her whole head of hair is made up of these small undesirable bits. The goal is to see that desirability is not inherent in an object or person. It's something the mind adds, as in, beauty is in the eye of the beholder. But when you do this exercise slowly, following this complex matrix, you really get it. Each body part required examination through all five senses, plus its form, the emotional arousal, karmic formations (think of this as like free-association), and consciousness thoughts. I worked on this about four or five hours a day for about a month.

"The weird thing happened when I started contemplating the buttocks of my imaginary woman. In the middle of my meditation, suddenly this small, hairy creature leapt out of my chest and thrust itself sexually at the image. It was a hallucination, but it seemed so vividly real I could actually see it. My awareness was so honed by the meditation, that when I turned it on this thing, I could make it hold still. It froze and stared back at me. It looked like Gollum from The *Lord of the Rings*, but covered with hair, a shriveled, little creature with spindly arms, short legs and hungry, obsessive eyes. I knew exactly what this was. I was looking at the true face of my lust. I felt overwhelmed with disgust, but also compassion for this poor wretched creature. I knew it was my fault he was this way, because I had repressed him for so many years, starved him. I told him I would be kinder to him in the future, and then said sternly that he would always be under my control. With a flicker, he shot back into my chest and disappeared."

I looked over at Josh. He was still propped on one elbow, staring at me. I paused in case he wanted to ask a question, but he just nodded slightly, signaling me to go on. This was getting into pretty bizarre territory. I tried to gauge how he was handling this, how well he could cope with what else I could say. Was I really going to tell him the whole story? I had not thought this through very well. Now that I was in the middle of it, the rest was going to unfold through its own momentum. There was no way to edit out the next chapter. Was it even appropriate for him to hear about it? Suddenly I was scared. If I kept going, it would change everything he knew and thought about me. I realized I had no idea how he was going to react.

"It's one thing, Josh, to penetrate reality and glimpse the

illusion. It's another thing to pierce the skin of your own orange, and find a mythic-psychic monster of your own making lurking there. Strangely, this hallucination was the most real thing about myself I had ever encountered. It forced me to recognize this tension that existed between the spiritual quest, this desire I had to know the world, and my need for women and sex. It seemed I had to give up one in order to get the other. I had broken up with my girlfriend in Canada before leaving for India. I had some great relationships on the road, including ecstatic tantric experiences. And also some really sour ones. I realized, though, that life in a monastery or as a wandering monk was not going to work for me and my Gollum. I wanted to find a woman who I could share the whole journey with.

"And then I met your mother."

The Wolf

"I met your mother near the end of my two years' travelling. She was teaching English in Xian, China. I fell in love–not so much with her, I guess, but with the romantic story of her as an American teacher who spoke Chinese and Japanese, and who, like me, loved the adventure of living in Asia. We traveled through China together for two weeks during her winter break. When we parted, I was determined to marry her. I proposed when I returned to Xian a month later after visiting Tibet. We got married that summer in the US, then went back to China to teach English together. A year later we moved to Japan and lived there for two and a half years. I was crazy about your mom when I met her, and she told me I was not like other men she had known. I felt that in marrying her, sex and love would never be a problem for me again, that it was all settled. I remember lying in her arms when we were first together and crying at one point, because I felt this overwhelming sense that she was going to love me and take care of me for the rest of my life. I felt–relief.

"But shortly after we were married, like within weeks, she

stopped responding to me sexually..."

Josh covered his ears, "Lalalala."

"Sorry, Josh, there's just no other way to tell this part."

"Look Dad, I think I know where this is going. When you and I were fighting a few years ago, before I moved out of your house, I had kind of figured out already that you had cheated on mom and this was what split you two up. So it was no real surprise when it came up. I confronted you then, asked with how many women? 'Tons,' you yelled at me. 'I slept with tons of women.'"

"I was exaggerating."

"It's not about the *volume*, Dad."

"Look, do you want me to tell you the story, or do you want me to stop? I can stop if you like. Sincerely, I mean it."

He paused. "Okay, I want you to tell me."

"All right. Suffice it to say, it was bad for both of us. I resented your mom bitterly for our lack of sex. After three years of being really unhappy, on a trip back to Canada I had a brief affair with an old girlfriend. I told your mom about it when we were back together, and I said maybe we should get divorced. To my astonishment, she became aroused."

"That really doesn't make any sense," he said warily.

"At the time I just didn't question it. Looking back, I think we were both in so much pain, the intensity just turned into desire. Even in the midst of it, it felt so fucked up. I felt like I was just being sucked in for another round of hurt. But I couldn't help myself. Within the month of this brief bliss, you were conceived. And then, it was as if a wall of black ice descended. We did not even know she was pregnant, but suddenly your mom was furious at me for my infidelity. She wanted nothing to do with me again, sexually. I felt she hated me. I felt trapped. I had a kid on the way, and a marriage that I couldn't fix.

"It was during this period that I had a psychic break. I had a job in Tokyo writing a monthly column for an English language magazine, informing ex-pats about the alternative spirituality scene in the city. One month I went for an interview and a free therapy session with this Californian-trained, Japanese Jungian Shaman. His approach to therapy was to try and unlock what the unconscious mind wants to say to the conscious mind. How perfect for me, right? In the middle of this session, I suddenly remembered a dream I had had when I was six years old. He asked me to tell him about it. In the dream, I had a little golden cage on my bedside table. In this cage was what looked like a little pet monkey, except it had pointed ears and fangs like a gremlin. I loved my little pet, so I opened the cage to pat it. But it bit me. I looked down at my hand and saw blood. When I looked up, I saw it had jumped out of the cage and was running out of my room. I felt a jolt of fear. I knew it was going into my parents' room. It was going to hurt my mom and dad. So I jumped out of bed. Too late, I remembered the wolves...

"When I was a kid I was afraid that wolves lived under my bed. During the day they were kept behind an invisible grating, but at night, the grating opened up, and they prowled around. I knew that if I let a foot slip over the edge, they would drag me under and devour me. In the dream, I looked down at my foot as it hit the floor and saw a wolf's head jut out from the bed and grab my ankle. At just this point as I was telling the therapist this dream, and I was fully reliving in my body as I was talking, he grabbed my ankle hard and said: 'Like this?'

"Josh, it was like an earthquake split my psychic crust apart. I felt this thing come rushing up through the crack. My whole body tensed up, and I could feel this dark, angry presence inside me, struggling to speak.

"The therapist saw the change instantly.

" 'Who are you?' he said to me.

" 'The wolf,' a deep, harsh voice croaked out of me as if I could barely speak.

" 'What do you want?'

" 'To…kill…Tim.'

" 'Why?'

" 'Because…he has kept me…locked…away.'

" 'Are you in there too Tim?' the therapist asked.

"I nodded. My conscious mind was still there. By this point in my life, I had experienced enough weird psychic shit that I could stay calm and just let it just happen. Gradually the Jungian drew the wolf into a dialogue with my conscious self, so that it and I were talking back and forth. He brokered a deal between what felt like two parts of my soul, between the conscious, controlling, linear left side of my brain, and the silent, vengeful right. The therapist helped the wolf see that if he killed me, he would die too. The wolf said he would let me live, but only if I agreed to let him out.

" 'But what does that mean?' I asked my other self.

" 'You know what that means,' he said with a snarl, and disappeared inside of me.

"The therapist and I talked about what happened. Because he was a Jungian, he could frame it in terms of the Shadow, the repressed parts of ourselves we can't accept that are literally forced underground into the unconscious. They don't go away though, and can surface as destructive behavior that seems to come out of nowhere. My first inclination, however, was to see it through my old Christian mythology, as a simple case of demon possession. It felt like a separate thing in me. But at the same time it felt like me. This was my bedside gremlin, my Gollum, now grown too powerful to keep under lock and key. I believed this thing when it said it wanted to kill me. Suddenly I understood Dr. Jekyll and Mr. Hyde, why it is that nice guys "go postal" and start shooting strangers. And most of all, I felt I understood the myth of the werewolf. That was my story now. That beast was in me, and was me. I was terrified.

"The Jungian therapist invited me to attend a Shamanic retreat he was conducting a few weeks later. I showed up and discovered I was the only 'foreign devil' in a room full of New-Agey Japanese. The Jungian found someone to translate for me. She was an attractive Japanese woman. Her English wasn't great, but that wasn't a problem, because most of the time we spent beating drums, dancing, and having lucid dreams to enter the spirit world. I describe it in a way that sounds a bit crazy, a bit silly, and it seemed pretty far up in the ozone layer even to me. But I got it that the point was to shake city folk out of daily reality through rhythm and movement, and to loosen our minds from the grip of everyday reality. After a few hours of this, the Jungian, now in full Shaman mode, told us to lie down on the floor in preparation for a session of lucid dreaming.

"We were supposed to imagine a cave in our minds, go through it into the underworld, find an animal spirit guide and ask it a question. I followed directions and soon found myself in a vast underground forest. I was a walking skeleton in the dream, living bones hiking through my own private netherworld. There was a cave inside that forest, and inside that cave, there they were, waiting for me. Six of them, sitting in a semicircle."

"Who?" said Josh. He was sitting up now, cross legged, staring straight in my eyes.

"My wolves. The ones who lived underneath my bed.

"I stepped towards them. Following the teacher's instructions, I asked permission to ask them a question. They laughed at me, jeering. They closed the circle round me. I saw jagged teeth flash. In an instant they were on me, tearing my bones apart. In a panic, I cried out to Jesus for help. And you know what, Josh? Jesus came to me. He entered the scene, lowered down into it, hanging on a cross. The wolves immediately turned on him. They attacked, eating his guts as he hung there. I knew he wasn't going to save me. I looked in Jesus' eyes, and his eyes said back to me like a spoken voice: 'This too is necessary–for you.'

"Then the wolves turned back on me. This time I surrendered to them. I did not panic, just let them crunch up my bones and devour them. As they devoured me I felt myself becoming them. I felt myself eating my own bones and then howling in a circle as we finished. Then a drum beat changed rhythm. It was a signal we were supposed to return from the dream to the waking world.

"We sat in a circle and everyone shared their experiences:

" 'My spirit guide was an eagle, he told me to be strong and soar.'

" 'My spirit guide was a turtle, she told me never give up.'

" 'My spirit guide was a pack of wolves, and I am going to hell...'

"At the end of the evening, as we headed out of the room to our dorm rooms, a harsh voice spoke in my head.

" 'No,' I said.

" 'You promised I could live. Now it's time.'

" 'But I don't know how to do this.'

" 'You don't have to do anything. Just step aside.'

"Suddenly, I was a different person. My wolf was in charge. He walked over to the pretty Japanese woman who had translated for me and asked if she would like to go for a walk. She said yes.

"She and I walked along a path through the woods surrounding the retreat center. I was screaming inside. I'm only lucky, desperately lucky, Josh, that this thing in me that I feared so much had not been locked up for a dozen more years. I understood then what it could be like for a man to become a rapist, even a murderer. And I marvel at the judgment of this therapist for letting me out of his sight once this dark thing was unleashed. What happened was this: the wolf spoke to her in my voice, my own reasonable tones. He told her about my strange experience in the therapy session. He told her about the wolves in the cave in my dream and my unhappy marriage. He said that what the wolf in me wanted was sex. How would she like to get a hotel room together for the night?

" 'This is therapy, right?' she asked.

"I nodded.

"She thought for a moment, in the silence, in the woods. 'Okay,' she said.

"We walked to the road, caught a cab, found a hotel and had sex. Just like that. At dawn we returned to the workshop center together, slipping into our dorm rooms as if nothing had happened. After that weekend, I never saw her again.

"This began my double life as a philanderer. Before, I always felt so awkward with women I was attracted to. I thought that if one was good enough, kind enough, harmless enough, then they would feel safe enough to have sex. But the wolf turned out to be very effective at directly seducing women. He was very good at picking the ones who found this approach attractive. The wolf explained my situation. Married with a pregnant wife, but unhappy in a sexless relationship. He was dispassionately honest. He was also economical. He didn't want to sleep with a lot of women, just a few who, for reasons of their own, liked having a private lover.

"When I was with your mom, I just totally walled this part off from my consciousness. We went for sonograms, moved back to Canada, got an apartment, my first book got published and I was doing TV interviews about my experience living in a Buddhist monastery, and what spiritual wisdom I had gleaned from my years living in Asia. In the middle of this came the most beautiful moment in my life. You were born. Your mother said to me during those days how glad she was that I was no longer so obsessed about having sex. I remember despising her then: for not seeing me, for not seeing any of what was going on in me.

"My lack of integrity was killing me, and I didn't know what to do. About five months after you were born, your mom accused me of having an affair with a woman friend of mine. Ironically, this was a woman I was not sleeping with. At first I indignantly denied it. But then I blurted out the truth that I had had affairs. It was an ugly scene. In my mind, I thought somehow she and I would work this through together. I told her I would stop. I put the wolf back in the cage and we went into couples therapy. A few months later she took you to Washington DC to visit her parents. When she arrived there, she called and told me she was not coming back. She had planned this for months, she said. She had left me.

" 'I don't want anything from you,' she told me. 'What you really want is to travel again, isn't it? Well, you can do that now. Travel the world, screw other women, I don't care. Just leave us alone. I don't need any child support. We're okay with my family.'

"That night I took a long bath. I remember lying in the warm water and thinking about your mom's words. The wolf had won me my freedom. It had chewed off a foot to free itself from a trap. I thought about the divorced men I knew who had children they hardly ever saw. There was a hollow look about these men. I thought about you, seven months old, crawling around, exploring, so full of laughter. How it felt to hold you in my arms. I knew I couldn't do it. I could not just walk away. I needed to be with you, to live out this love I had for you. There was no other life for me. I knew it would kill something in me if I didn't.

"So I left Canada, drove down to Washington, moved in with your mother and her parents, and tried to reconcile. She didn't want me there. They didn't want me there. But once I was in their house, they couldn't throw me out. I had next to no money and could not legally work in the US. So I took care of you half the time and the rest of the time worked on a second book in a room at a neighbor's house. Your mom and I talked and argued and fought, trying to find some way we could live together. This was the hardest period of my life, Josh. I had no friends, no job, and I lived in shame every day. I had made a promising start of a career as a writer in Canada, but that was 500 miles away now. We've been talking about how our story builds the structure of our self. I had had this wild, Jungian narrative of my wolf, my shadow, my dark side. But strip away the story, and I was just living out the predictable consequences of adultery and betrayal."

"Dad?" Josh had been silent a long time, just taking this in. This was the first time he had said a word in half an hour. "You know, it was a bit scary to hear you speak in the voice of the wolf just now. I could feel it alive in you when you were talking. I remember when I was a kid, if you wanted to scare me, sometimes you would give me this look. Then you would move really slowly in this certain menacing way. It would really freak me out."

"I remember."

"You know, I do this with my little brother sometimes, when he's bugging me. I give him this look, and I start to move real slow towards him. He begs me to stop. And I remember too that when I was little, I was never scared of anything except after I watched that werewolf movie with Mom and her second husband."

"Oh yeah, I remember." I said. "You were terrified after that movie that werewolves would come in through your bedroom window at night. I told you werewolves were fictional, but that didn't help. Then I explained your window was too small and too high up and if anything came in the ground floor I would kill it myself before it could ever get you."

"Yeah, that didn't help either."

"Okay, but good parenting moment for me that I didn't say: 'Don't worry Josh, I'm a werewolf too. I know all about them. I'll protect you from the others.' "

"Oh, yeah, Dad, excellent job with that one!" he laughed.

"I want to tell you about one thing I remember when I first got to Washington after your mom left me. You were nine months old by then, just starting to walk. I couldn't believe I had missed seeing you learn how to stand. When I came into your grandparents' house, I held out my arms, but you wouldn't hug me. You wouldn't come near me, as if you were afraid of me. But you couldn't take your eyes off me either. You followed me around, still unsteady on your feet. I could tell you knew who I was. I was this person who was always in your life but who suddenly disappeared for eight weeks, an eternity for a toddler. I remember feeling this distrust and attraction all mixed together. It was killing me. So I took off my belt and threw one end to you. You grabbed it and we started playing tug of war. I pretended you were so strong. I struggled, but in the end you pulled me over. We both started laughing. We must have played this game for half an hour, gradually getting closer to each other on the belt, until at the end you dropped the belt and let me hug you."

I wiped my face.

"So now I was living in your grandparents' house, amongst the people I had hurt most. Your grandmother hated my guts. She would make me weed her vegetable garden and stand over me like some Alabama prison guard. I imagined her with a cowboy hat and reflective silver sunglasses, the hot sunlight gleaming off the barrel of her shotgun. If I ever disagreed with her, she'd spit out: 'You're just a man who can't keep it in his pants!'

"Your mom and I tried to make it work. But there was no way past the hurt and betrayal. To make a very long story short, after three months I moved out of your grandparents' house and into a rented basement room nearby. I went on taking care of you in their home half the time every day as your mom and I kept talking. Eventually, she told me she wanted a divorce. Like a complete moron, I was totally surprised when she filed for sole child custody. As a writer, I had adapted my schedule to taking care of you half the time, which I wanted to continue. She wanted me to have you on Wednesdays and every other weekend, but not overnight. She did not think it was safe to leave you alone with me. I decided to fight for joint custody.

"What I would like you to imagine, Josh, is what it was like to have this story of the wolf, which I had tried to explain to your mom during our couples therapy, replayed in a courtroom. Imagine her lawyer has me on the stand. He runs through the details of my affairs, which I have admitted under deposition.

"Then he says: 'And you have said that you were possessed by a wolf that made you do these things. Is that right?'

"My lawyer objects. But I want to answer.

" 'It's a *metaphor*,' I say. 'I'm a writer. I was trying to explain how I felt in a metaphor.'

"Your mother's surprise witness was our couples therapist, flown in from Ottawa for the hearing. I had to waive my patient-client privacy rights for her to testify, which I did. Your mom's lawyer pulled out of her all kinds of details of the Jungian weirdness I was going through. But this was a tactical mistake. At the end of the therapist's testimony, I wrote two questions for my lawyer to ask her in cross-examination.

" 'Would you say Mr. Ward's overall emotional state at the time that you worked with him falls within the normal range?'

" 'Yes.'

" 'Do you have any reason to believe he should not have joint custody of his son?'

" 'No, no reason,' she shook her head.

"The judge concluded the hearing succinctly: 'Well, Mr. Ward's behavior clearly shows he was a lousy husband and didn't care about his wife. But that's no reason for the court to believe he's incapable of being a good father. The court doesn't award custody. It can only take it away. In this case we see no justification to take custody away from him.'

"The judge put you on a week to week schedule. A week with your mom, a week with me. A year later your mom finally agreed to settle out of court and to continue on the schedule the judge imposed. That week-to-week schedule is, I suppose, all that you ever knew growing up.

"I want to add one final thing: this experience destroyed my story of myself as a Christo-Nietzsche-Buddhist-free-spirit guy, creating his life as he chooses. That story made me feel superior to other people. *I've* traveled the world, *I've* lived in a Buddhist monastery, *I've* embraced my dark side. In a sense, I was still filling my trophy case, creating a thick crust of a self that made me feel special. At age 33, living in a rented basement room with no job, no friends where I lived, a wrecked marriage and a child who I could not support, I had to face up to the fact that my life was in ruins. I was depressed, and my best plan was to get back into a sexless marriage with a woman who hated me for very good reasons. That was a huge gift, having my story so utterly, utterly destroyed. My family back in Ottawa and some old friends were incredibly supportive. They told me they loved me, without judgment, and even helped me pay my legal fees. My sister said it best. She told me, 'You know what's great about this mess? I think sometimes you think we love you because we admire all the things you've done, how smart you are. It's great to see you really fuck up, so you can get it that we love you for who you are, not for what you've done.' "

Josh snorted a laugh. I paused and we sat in silence for a minute. I was worried how he was taking all this. I knew he would need time just to process it. A part of me was already regretting every word I had said, wishing I could stuff it all back inside. The other part was just plain glad it was said.

"I just wanted you to know what happened, what made your life the way it was. The real story, as true as I can tell it. I didn't really mean to go into such detail, and I don't really know if I should have said anything about it at all... Did your mom ever tell you any of this stuff about the divorce?" I asked tentatively.

"Wow, no. Not like this."

"Well, look, I've got one final part of my story to tell. I'm getting hungry and stiff lying here all afternoon. Shall I tell it quick and then let's see if we can get a drink and a snack?"

Josh nodded, and I picked up where I left off.

Finding the Goddess

"When your mom and I finally split, I started dating again. I had no idea just how wounded I was. The wolf was out of his cage, but a very different creature. I could still be direct and seductive with women, but I could tell something was broken inside. I couldn't stand the idea that any one woman could make me so miserable again. So as soon as I was in a relationship, I started looking around for other women. I had become just the kind of guy I had despised in my Christian days.

"Then I met Teresa. She was a journalist. We met when she interviewed me about one of my books. On our first date I told her I thought monogamy was a delusion and I would never marry her. She laughed. 'Who asked you to?' she said. Teresa really enjoyed the intensity of the wolf in me. But she could also tell I was damaged goods. She never saw me as more than a fling. As the fling extended into years, my destructive patterns got worse. The closer I felt to her, the more determined I was to seek out other women, as if to prove to myself I was not going to fall back into the cage. Eventually she was ready to call it quits with me over this. I'm minimizing the struggle here, but I couldn't stand to lose her. I realized that what going on in me was more than just a bruised man trying to get over his divorce.

"While a normal guy might have just gone for therapy, I decided to dig into my dysfunction with women by writing a book. It took me six years. To write *Savage Breast: One Man's Search for the Goddess* I went back to Europe, this time to explore all the places where the Goddess was worshiped, to Greece, Rome, Crete, Cyprus, Turkey. It was fascinating for me to go back to some of the places I had seen as a Christian in my early twenties, but this time with the totally different perspective. Now I was digging beneath the layers of Christianity for an older, lost narrative. Studying ancient mythology led me into the world of

Jungian archetypes and the anima–the inner feminine within men. I took a shovel to my own psyche and exhumed old feelings and unconscious attitudes towards the feminine that were buried real deep. It took years to dredge all this stuff into my awareness, and then to write it all out in a close to intelligible shape. The book did okay. But the point is, doing this work, and doing it with Teresa, who stuck with me through it all, changed my story of myself and my relationships with women. I was able to dismantle the isolated, bitter myth of the wolf and recognize in it my own fracture with my inner feminine. I felt connected to life again, like I did when I was a Christian, but a new mythology, one without the sin and guilt. Teresa and I have been married seven years now. It's the longest I have ever been with one woman. I still look around and find myself grateful, every day, for the life I have right now."

"But it's still just a story, right?"

I laughed.

"You know, Josh, it's always hard to remember that life as we live it now is just the current narrative. Yes, it's just a story. But to me it's a *great* story."

Sully called us for dinner. We crawled outside and stretched in the fading sunlight. We washed up with our bowls of steaming water then made our way to the green tent.

"Mmmm, tuna stew. What a change," I said.

"Actually, the peppers, the onions, it's pretty tasty," said Josh. The cook's really done a great job tonight."

I had been talking for over two hours. Now I felt the silence between us as we ate. Finally Josh broke the tension.

"I remember sitting on the stairs when I was little, hearing you and Mom yelling at each other. I just went in the next room and, I dunno, bounced around. But I have these little memories, of like, you and Mom at my grandparents' house. I don't remember what you said, I just remember the tone of voice. I've got like four or five little snippets. That's all I remember.

"I never remember thinking of you and Mom as having once been together, and then divorced. I had seen friends' parents who lived in the same house, going out for the evening, and of course parents as couples on TV. So I guess I subconsciously must have known that other parents love each other. But I never connected it to you and Mom. I just knew that you were my dad, she was my mom, you guys didn't like each other, and that was okay. Somehow I was there, and somehow you two were hand-selected, as if someone said, 'Okay you are going to be Josh's dad and you are going to be Josh's mom. Here's the schedule, now work it out.

"So I guess I never really wondered why you got divorced. Later, when I was a teenager, I knew it must have something to do with adultery–"

"Did she–"

"No," he interrupted. "Mom didn't tell me. I sort of figured it out."

I started to jump in again, far from convinced that she had said nothing, but he held up a hand and spoke over me.

"But what I want to *say* now, Dad, is that I've held that against you for a long time. To me, there is nothing worse than betrayal. You know I have had girlfriends cheat on me. It hurt so bad. It's the worst thing there is. It made me see you differently, a little differently. Like that was something about you I just didn't think I'd be able to let go of. I didn't expect you to know or care what I felt. But hearing what you said this afternoon, it gave me a glimpse into the fucked up world you were in then. I guess it reminded me of your humanity."

He paused and looked me straight in the eye. "I just want you to know, now that you've told me your story, I forgive you, Dad."

After so much talking, I was at a loss for words, as if my throat had closed shut. I hadn't known he had held this against me. I never expected forgiveness. Not from his mother, not from anyone. It never hit me before how much I needed to hear those words. But there was something I couldn't accept about it. Josh had borne the consequences of our divorce. He had the right to forgive me for that. But this was not what he was offering. He couldn't forgive me for wrongs against his mother. A piece of me wanted to argue about it. But the force of the feeling behind his words was so strong, so definite. It was not an offer. He was forgiving me. It was an act, already finished in his mind. He cut me free, and for exactly this.

"Uh, thank you Josh," was all I could get out.

We stood up from the table at the same time, like two gunslingers ready to draw. He threw out his arms and the closed them around me, and I wrapped him in mine. I could feel myself sinking in, breathing deep, and relaxing into his embrace. We stood like this for a long time.

I tried to explain the destruction of my marriage to my father. I tried to tell him about my dark side, convinced that he who had failed to understand me all these years, could never comprehend this thing in me.

"Do you know your dark side?" I asked him.

"Of course I do," he said. "My brother."

Uncle John, my father's only sibling, was a stuttering schizophrenic, a man-child in a hulking, obese body. He lived alone in a smelly basement apartment where he kept stacks of yellowed newspapers and his stamp and coin collections. John was fond of childish jokes and silly puns and had a savant-like knowledge of streetcar schedules. He went in and out of psychiatric treatment centers and talked about killing himself from time to time. It seemed to be a plea for attention. To be in the presence of his brother was, I believe, physically painful for my father. He saw in John everything he feared: a life without purpose or productivity, needy and weak. It was made worse by the fact that my grandmother lavished all her poisonous, possessive care on John, her wounded son, and left my father to fend for himself.

After my grandmother died in the early 1990s, Uncle John's health improved. He lost weight and he started speaking to me about a girlfriend he met at one of the several groups he attended for people with mental disabilities. But he died just a few years later in his early fifties. The Toronto police called my parents' house. They had found John on a park bench one winter morning. He had fallen asleep outside and died of hypothermia. The police were calling it an accident. My father made arrangements for the funeral. I came up to Toronto from Washington to help empty the apartment and to attend what would surely be a grim and lonely little ceremony at a local funeral hall.

People entered. Strange people none of our family knew. Many of them looked kind of odd. They kept coming, filling the hall, greeting each other like friends. The attendant put out more chairs. Fifty, seventy five, maybe a hundred people, I lost count. These were John's friends from all the groups and half-way houses where he had spent his time. They gave us their condolences and spoke of how much John had meant to them. He was always so cheerful. He had such a sense of humor. He never had a bad word to say about anyone. He was always so ready to help out, or just lend a listening ear.

"You must really miss him," they said to us, and squeezed our hands.

Chapter Seven

Entering the Dead Zone

Day Five: Karanga Valley to Barafu Camp (4,673 meters) 4 kilometers

We awoke to a thick layer of frost on our tent. This was to be another short trekking day which would bring us to the base of the summit. We had 600 meters elevation to gain, back to the height of the Lava Tower that had caused Josh such pain. I hoped he had acclimatized. This evening we would wake before midnight to begin the eight-hour climb to the peak. The path ahead of us was strewn with scree, rubble and clumps of lava. No more scrubby grasses, no more brilliant bouquets of white everlastings. Except for a few random splotches of lichen, this was a dead zone.

"How did you sleep, Dad?"

"Not well. I had insomnia most of the night, but just resting was good for me. It gave me time to think about our conversation yesterday," I said as we headed off on a long level ridge. "I wanted to tell you my story so you could understand me better, and maybe understand yourself better too. But you know, I also came out of it with a different sense of why we need to tell our stories. Remember when I started talking about the selfplex and how we can brick ourselves in with stories that define us? It's almost like we build a tower, and inside that tower we are alone. So when we share our stories, it's like inviting someone else into the tower."

"Like Rapunzel?"

"Yes," I said with a laugh. Josh had been in a production of *Into the Woods* in the spring, so fairy tale memes were obviously fresh in his mind. "We let down our long hair, and this other person climbs into our tower. Through listening to another person's stories, you get to experience his or her subjective reality, see how the world looks from inside their tower. So anyway, I had this idea that we would talk about memes and technology today. I want to let go of all that for now, and ask instead if you would tell me your story. I'd like to hear it."

"Um, I've never really thought about my life story," he said. "You know, bits and pieces to girlfriends and friends. But nothing like you did yesterday."

"Hey, I know the basic plot. What I want to hear is what it was like to be you, growing up the way you did."

He took a deep breath.

"Okay, well... A lot of my earliest memories are from you and me living at the farm and Mom and me living at the condo. I remember there were a lot of people on the farm. I didn't really feel a connection to them, though, as if we were a family. I remember my bedroom with the glass bird feeder on the outside of the window. I remember my bed, with all the alphabet letters surrounding it. You going over those letters with me every night, making the cards with words on them and stuff.

"All the stories of the Little Mouse that we told in the car rides back and forth from school, these are some of my most vivid memories. When I think about it, the Little Mouse was my inner subconscious, I guess. Through him I could do things I could never do in real life. I could do whatever I wanted, 'cause I was this mouse with a magic back pack. That's a lot of what I love about acting, how you get to really experience this infinite variety you would never get in real life. This was my start with that. It was such a freeing experience.

"I remember Mom's house was usually pretty quiet. We'd spend time together. Mostly we'd draw or I'd watch Japanese cartoons or videos. Sometimes she'd light some incense. We'd kind of meditate, sit and chill. She'd make pudding. It was just the two of us. We'd stay up late on the Fourth of July and do sparklers. I used to kick the soccer ball back and forth across the room for hours. I could not get enough of kicking that ball.

"My friends thought it was really strange that I lived in two houses. But I liked it. I was used to it. Some of my friends stayed in the same house all their lives. How boring, I thought. At the end of every week I packed up my stuff. If you are moving that often you can't take that much with you. You can't get too attached to things. So I learned to pack light and be happy with the bare minimum. You moved houses five times. Mom moved three times. Maybe this is why I'm really comfortable traveling to strange places, because I can adapt quickly. I can be anywhere and just not worry about it.

"I felt like this particle flying through space. There was never this cohesive family, this grounded home. There was just me, drifting from place to place. Two of my best friends in elementary school moved back to their home countries, and it was okay. I knew nothing was permanent. You were there, Mom was there. I think that's all the grounding I have. To me it wasn't difficult or strange. That was how I was comfortable.

"The great thing was, I had dogs, both at the farm with you and with Mom at the house when she remarried. I felt so connected to animals. I think it might be because I was always surrounded by grownups and grownup talk. There weren't really kids or siblings. I felt more like I was one of these other entities. Whenever anything was wrong at school or with you guys and I felt lonely, I could just go and be with my dogs."

"I remember when you were three, you were always pretending to be a dog" I jumped in. "You would bark a lot, and stick out your tongue as if you were panting. We'd go for a walk together, and it was very convenient, because I could just call heel and you would come running," I laughed. "I got some strange stares in shopping malls."

"I changed schools a couple of times, and I didn't have a lot of constant friends, just my two best friends, Josh R. and Adam. I acted up a lot in class. I guess I loved being the goofy one."

He told a story about getting in trouble in school for writing his initials on the carpet in class.

"But Josh, when you talk about acting out, you did have this period when you were about nine when you got so hostile I took you this therapist to try to find out what was going on. What was happening then?"

"I vaguely remember this. You took me to this lady who wanted to play with toys and draw and talk about my life. I didn't like her."

"After the first session she showed me a drawing of a tree you did for her. She pointed to these three black oval knotholes you had put in the trunk. She said these represented holes in your heart. I think what she meant by this is that these are places where you were really hurt inside. It hit me hard. I felt a lot of guilt. Was I refusing to see negative stuff in your life, the life in two houses I had forced on you? Those knotholes became symbolic for me–the dark shaded parts of you that I could not see..."

"Seriously, Dad?" Josh laughed. "You know when I was that age I watched *The Bob Ross Art Show* on TV. I remember him painting a 'happy little tree' with knotholes. He explained to the audience that real trees aren't all smooth and flawless. So I made it a point to put a knothole or three in every single tree I drew. I'd draw entire Swiss-tree forests."

"Well, whack me in the head. I sure got that all wrong."

"Yeah. I just remember I felt pretty happy most of the time. I do remember when my mom and her new husband started fighting I spent a lot of time in my room, playing with my Legos. Or I would bring some blankets under the dining room table, a flashlight, some books and candy. I would make a fort and stay there for hours. I remember it felt really good to be in there, but looking back I think, hmm... You know, I never made a fort at any other point in my life."

"Doesn't that say a lot, though?" I added. "It's like you were saying, 'I am going to make a place for myself that's safe and fun, and I can shut out the negative stuff that's going on around me.' There's a double edge here Josh, if to stay happy you have to tune out the painful things that happen around you."

We stopped talking for a while as we labored to climb a steep hill. I felt the dryness in my throat as the air rasped in and out of my heaving chest. I was breathing as if I was running hard, not walking up a sloping hill. It felt like my lungs were not getting all the oxygen they needed in order to power my straining leg muscles.

Josh saw me wheezing a bit. "Hey, remember the Alexander Technique."

I relaxed, tried to just tilt slightly forward so I could fall up the hill, and use minimum effort in my legs to glide forward with each step.

He spoke now in bursts between breaths about high school and his first four girlfriends. My own relationships with women had been so painful, especially with his mother, that I had often worried about him falling into similar traps.

"...Looking back," he said, "I found that when I had a girlfriend I focused a lot of my energy on her and let other things fall by the wayside. I kept feeling this sense of freedom every time I had a breakup. I'd hang out with friends and do stuff again. So I resolved after high school I would never lose myself in a relationship again, and always maintain that inner relationship with myself. Maybe I was throwing myself into new relationships too much because I never had anything like this before. I don't know if that had anything to do with you and Mom. I guess I never got to see a mature emotional relationship. I certainly never saw it with Mom and her second husband, and I didn't know what the hell you and Teresa were. What was she doing here? Why were we suddenly moving into her house?

Nobody explained."

My heart sank. So after this decade-long struggle to heal my emotional wounds and create this deep bond with the love of my life, my son–living in the same house with Teresa and me for five years–says he's never seen a mature emotional relationship. Well, it was too late now. What was I going to say: read my book on the subject?

We took a water break, leaning against some lava boulders. They had been warmed by the sun, and felt good to touch.

"Do you want to say anything about the issues you and I had because of your relationship with Tiffani?"

"It's funny you still talk about it that way. Mostly it was because of the grades and everything that caused the negative way I started to see you in high school. But yeah, I couldn't understand why you didn't like Tiffani. I know she was two years younger than me, and in some ways quite immature. But I was in love with her, so why shouldn't you be? You just went quiet every time I said something about her. I felt that you were so wrong. It was such a weird thing for me because usually if you'd say something, I'd see something differently and I'd go, 'Oh, it's so true!' But I'd never felt that anything you ever said to me before that was that wrong. I mean, for you I faced the rooster."

"It's true I didn't like her," I jumped in. "Immature? She looked and acted like a twelve-year-old. You were seventeen, but you seemed to regress to her age when you were together. You even picked up her habit of twirling the ends of your hair. Not a pretty meme. I didn't like any of it, but I could live with it. It was your choice. What terrified me though was that you were so insistent you two were not having sex. I thought if it happened, you would not be protected and she could get pregnant."

"Here's the thing, Dad. Looking back, I really get you were trying to protect me from all this. From a parental standpoint, yes, this was valid. But from a *me* standpoint, I am so happy I went through that relationship, because no matter how much you could have guided me, I would not know what I know as deeply as I do if I had not gone through it. I needed to make stupid decisions and I needed to be wrong and I needed to really honestly truly believe something and have it be completely shattered. My gut instincts had been telling me all along after a certain point that I needed to end it, and I was just pushing it back in my mind. If I had just said, 'Okay Dad, you are right,' and broke it off in the first week, I wouldn't have learned what I needed. I don't feel like any of that time was wasted or regretted. I enjoyed our relationship. I did have a lot of fun with her. Sure, in the end she cheated on me. But what relationship doesn't end badly? Everyone has a billion things like that happen.

"Massage school was another big part of this because you were saying, 'No, no, there's no way I'm going to support this. Going straight to college is the best thing.' I felt you were trying to stop me from making what you thought was a stupid decision. That was a real turning point for me. It was a big step towards my independence, realizing that my parents are human and that they can be wrong, too. That was my moment where I got to say, 'I respect your opinion, but this is what I'm going to do.' Now, I've got a job that I really enjoy. I make a lot of people happy. You probably most of all, with your thirty billionth massage."

"Yeah, that is true," I admitted. "It's not the massage school I objected to though. It's just that I thought you were doing it as an excuse not to go to college so you could live at your mom's and be close to Tiffani."

"That's not the way it was," Josh said, and clamped his jaw shut. He marched ahead for a while in silence.

"I had three or four things I just did not want to talk to you about that last year of school," he continued. "All you wanted to talk to me about was grades and colleges. It was like nothing else I did was pleasing you. I felt I could not stand being in your house any more. The more you would grind on me about grades, the more I would resist. I didn't want you to think that your making me miserable was having a positive effect on my grades."

We crested a hill. I stopped to catch my breath, in order to respond. I was getting kind of angry, because Josh was not remembering some details exactly as they happened. At least as I remembered them happening. I was aware we had both edited the experience to fit our personal narratives. I watched him tilt his head back and drink deep from his water bottle. He wiped the water from his cracked lips. His gaze shifted behind me, into the distance.

"Wow."

I looked around, and saw a whole new mountain. This was our first glimpse of Mawenzi, Kilimanjaro's other peak, which had been hidden from our view until this point by Kibo's massive cone. At 5,149 meters, Mawenzi is smaller than Kibo, but harder to climb. The crater has these long pointed shafts of hardened lava sticking straight up. It looks like a lower jaw full of sinister, jagged teeth. According to my guidebook, when Mawenzi's volcanic cone was formed, molten magma flowed into the vertical cracks and crevices of the crater's rim. The lava hardened, and in the subsequent ages the softer rock eroded by wind and rain, leaving behind only sinister-looking pinnacles and serrated edges of the lava.

We were near to our camp now. Fred told us to keep walking, as lunch would be waiting when we arrived. So we bottled the rest of the conversation and put the remainder of our energy into crossing the last valley and up a ridge to Barafu Camp. As we approached, we could see the Mweka trail join with ours. Four of the six routes to the top converged here for the final ascent. The path began to look like a caravan route, with a steady stream of porters loaded down with gear. Many of them carried large plastic containers filled with water. Barafu has no springs or streams, so water all had to be carried in from water sources lower down. Our private toilet would not be brought up to the camp, Fred said, as the porters were not able to haul up the extra water for cleaning it. We would be forced to resort to the communal outhouses.

The rocky ridge of Barafu had fewer flat spaces than our previous camps, so the tents were spread out all along the last half mile of the trail like a crowded shantytown. Hundreds of porters laughed and joked with each other in large clumps. Gear bags were strewn everywhere. Among them we spotted a steel rescue stretcher by the green rangers' hut. I could not fathom what it would take to carry someone down from the peak. If the problem was AMS, then being carried lower would do the trick. But if one broke a neck or back, what use would a stretcher be? I asked Fred about helicopter rescue. He said there was a landing pad twelve kilometers away. A chopper would then have to be called in from Nairobi.

We found our tent at the high end of the ridge near where the climb to the peak began. It was just a short walk away from three outhouses. They balanced over the edge of a precipice, nailed to some boards for support. Fred told us to not walk around in search of them at night without a flashlight, or we might fall over the edge. We could not see the summit from the camp, but we could feel it in the occasional gusts of wind that brought the icy air of the glaciers rattling through the tents.

To our delight, we found Marita and Bastian camped nearby. We had not seen them since the morning of day three, as their faster schedule put them ahead of us. We embraced each other like long-lost friends. They had climbed the summit the previous night, and had only returned a few hours ago. Their faces were crimson with sunburn. They looked exhausted. It had been a hard walk, they told us. The wind had been bitterly cold.

"Wear every piece of clothing you've got," Bastian told us.

"My AMS was real bad," said Marita. "I had nausea during the climb. I vomited in the dark."

"But she kept going," said Bastian, his voice full of respect.

"We saw another trekker have some kind of seizure," she

jumped back in. "He was flailing his arms and freaking out. One of his guides had to grab him and hold him down, pinning his arms to keep him from falling and hurting himself."

"Imagine how hard for the guides," said Bastian, looking up the hillside and speaking in his passionless Terminator voice. "You have to fight the rich tourist who is paying you to do your job. They have walked for a week to reach the top. Now you have to tell them, go back, you are too sick. Very difficult," he shook his head.

Marita gave him a little kick with her boot. His eyes snapped to her and then back to us, as he realized what he was saying was not at all encouraging.

"Just remember, *pole, pole*," he concluded in a suddenly upbeat tone. "If you climb fast, that's when you get into trouble."

"But don't stop moving. Stopping is terrible," Marita added. "You're exhausted, but it is so hard to get started again."

Josh and I exchanged a worried glance.

"How long did it take you to reach the top?" Josh asked.

"About eight hours," said Bastian.

"Eight hours of just looking at nothing, seeing only the feet of the climber in front of you and freezing," Marita continued, eyes down, as if reliving the ordeal. "There are parts of it, climbing over shale, where for every two steps up you slide one step back. It was the most exhausting climb I ever had. And then you get to the top. You see the glaciers. You see the sun. We kissed on Uhuru Peak. We said to each other, 'You know, we climbed Kilimanjaro together. Whatever else happens in our marriage, we did this together. So we can survive anything.' "

They told us they still had a four-hour walk to the last campsite, where they would spend the night. They were all packed and had to leave right away. We hugged each other once more and waved them on their way.

"I'm so happy for Marita and Bastian," Josh said.

"They are still pretty young," I replied. "But maybe a possible example of the kind of relationship you were saying you never saw growing up. I hope we see them again."

Josh shot me a scared look.

"No, no, I don't mean it like 'I hope we survive.' I mean it like, 'I hope our paths cross again.' "

I laughed. But the laugh rang a little hollow.

Sully welcomed us to lunch. It consisted of slices of white bread, made into sandwiches that had been pan fried top and bottom with a bit of egg batter coating. We figured the cook might have been aiming for some hybrid of french toast and grilled cheese. With anticipation we took our first bite and discovered inside of them—nothing. We pulled the bread apart and spread peanut butter and jam on the insides, and enjoyed another totally unique meme of Tanzanian tourist cuisine. As we ate, Sully flitted around the tent like a moth with ADD. He knocked over the mustard jar as he fussed. He seemed more nervous than we were.

"Friend, Joshua, you headache, okay?"

"Actually, Sully it's back again. Not too bad, but I feel it again."

"Oh! You drink, drink!" he urged. "Papa, you drink too!"

We sipped our tea dutifully.

"I didn't know your headache was back," I said.

"Yeah. It was not so bad on the walk. I've been taking the pills all along and I've got a few more. I'll be okay."

Fred came into our tent with Frank, the assistant guide, whom we had not yet met. They would both accompany us to the summit. Fred told us to carry three liters each of water and to take whatever protein bars or snacks we had left with us. He said we should try to eat a little bit all the way along the trail to keep our energy up. He told us he would wake us at 11 p.m. We would have tea at 11:30 in the dinner tent, and then we would start the climb at midnight.

We settled into our tent for the rest of the afternoon, excited and anxious.

I thought about Rapunzel. Actually, it was a terrible metaphor. You get that other person in your tower, and in a sense you are taking them hostage, at least if you are just selling your story so that they will believe it too. It's just helping you reinforce your own walls. That's not real intimacy. I do want to know Josh's story, but I don't want to be seduced by the golden hair, the pretty side. I was glad we were finally discussing some of the stuff that led to our rift, I told myself, but there are places where his memory is just wrong. I guess I still want to be the wolf, in this case, the big bad wolf ready to huff and puff and, well, not to blow his whole tower down, but blow a few holes in the walls.

"You know, Josh, in terms of a mature relationship, what I guess I'd like you to know about me and Teresa is that we can tell each other our stories, and it's okay to challenge them, to point out the differences, the bullshit. With her, I know when she calls me on something it's because she doesn't want me to be caught up in my own story. It's not easy on your own to know when your story is helping you create a useful structure for living your life, and when it's just building a crust. She and I help keep an eye out for each other's blind sides. And it's okay for us to knock down each other's walls from time to time. It keeps us from getting stuck in a shtick. That's my idea of an intimate relationship. This is what I would really like to have with you."

"Okay," he said in an upbeat tone.

"Ah, it's so frustrating, Josh. Sometimes I don't know if you are getting what I'm saying or just want me to move on."

"I get it."

"So, do you want to carry on where we left off on the trail? It's really the point where your story and my story converge, right?"

He nodded and continued: "That last month I lived in your house, I just remember trying to be in my room as much as possible. Trying not to talk to you. Every Friday you'd check

Edline, and a thunderstorm would come down on my head: 'You've got a C, or a D instead of a B! How come this thing that you told me didn't line up with that thing on Edline?' Next week the teacher would phone you and say something, and you'd be mad at me again. It was just this mess. I just wanted to do it all myself and worry about it myself. I was screaming in my head, 'Let me fuck up! Let me do it!' I had the feeling that the only people who were really with me were Tiffani, my best friends, Mom to a degree. It really sucked not having you to talk to. I felt really lost and confused and stressed. It's not like the work I was turning in was bad, it's just that I wasn't turning some things in. I would see an assignment for a three-page paper and go, 'I just don't want to do it.' "

"Josh, there were consecutive weeks you just totally stopped doing all your work."

"It's not that I stopped. It's just that I didn't give a shit."

"Okay, but the result was that there were many assignments that you just didn't do. That's just not something common–"

"Really?" He laughed derisively, as if I were clueless about the realities of high school.

"No, it's not common. Not for a smart kid like you. Not unless you are a drug addict or clinically depressed. Remember we went to see your guidance counselor, you, me and your mom, and she said 'Josh, how can I explain to colleges your high SAT scores and your B- average?' You just shrugged at us."

"I was just at a really crappy point in my life, and it affected me. I realized while I was at Mom's house, I felt so free, and I could just do work. 'Cause, once this started to happen, Mom never mentioned homework, ever, to me, because I ranted about how much I hated it that you were doing it. I felt great at her house, and I felt like shit at yours. I felt this is what I need to do. Leave you, because I get stuff done over here."

"Josh, you are mixing up cause and effect. You stopped doing your work first–then I got hard on you. Not the other way around. And you make it sound like this was a one-time thing and I overreacted. But these were serious, potentially grade-failing lapses on your part. There were four distinct periods: spring of grade 10, fall 11, spring 11, fall grade 12. Grounding you and threatening to pull you out of plays were the only things that worked. I would watch, amazed, as in a week you would catch up on all the missed assignments, and even get good grades. It made me crazy. When I tried to find out if you were having problems, you would just feed me bullshit."

"Like what?" he asked angrily.

"Like when you told me you were biting yourself. That you had a self-biting problem."

"Oh, I remember that now," Josh laughed, his anger dissipated. "I was so mad, I was furious at you for grounding me again. I felt like hurting myself to get back at you. I remember biting myself on the arm, and thinking, this isn't working. I can't bite hard enough. I remember telling you about it, so you would relent, and inside, yelling at myself, 'Oh God, what am I saying? My arms don't even look bad! Who the hell would believe this crap!' "

"When you think about it, Josh, I always tried to guide, rather than draw strict boundaries. I just wanted to help set you up with some kind of a system that would keep you on track–"

"No, Dad. It was just a game of chicken you and I were playing. I was determined not to do anything that was going to prove your methods right. In my eyes, if you ever circled and highlighted in yellow 'That works!' then I felt I would be fucked for the rest of my life."

"I guess I kind of knew that," I half laughed. "But I honestly didn't know what else to do. I felt if I could just keep you in the game, next semester it might be different. Because if you drop, it's really hard to get back on board. You know, that's what happened to your mom. She told me she basically stopped going to classes in grade ten.

"Really?" Josh sounded surprised. "This is new information."

"Yeah. She only got into college for languages in the US because she went to Japan and studied there, then came back with a whole bunch of credits towards a degree. She told me, 'Maybe Josh is going through what I went through?' I said, 'And thank God you care more about his grades than your parents did.' She said, 'Yes, I do care more than my parents did.' It was one of the few times she and I really worked together as a team."

I shifted on my sleeping bag to look at the blue fabric overhead. The wind was up again, and shivering the whole tent frame.

"You know, Josh, you said your mom backed off you, that you only felt pressure at my house. Did you know she was forwarding me the teachers' notes and faxing me the school letters about your failing grades? I wondered then, and I wonder now, did she set me up for a confrontation with you? Was it her idea that you should get away from me?"

I could feel the edge in my own voice, despite my effort to control it.

"No, it was my idea. She only backed off after you and I split.

"That's not what you just said a minute ago."

"Then that was not what I meant."

"So where did you find out that legally you could choose to leave my house?"

"I forget where I found out. Online I guess. It was such a shock to me. My life had always been dictated that it was going to be a week here and week there–"

"Was it something Tiffani told you?"

"No. After I told her about it, she just said, 'I just want what's going to make you happiest.' "

I wanted to argue. I wanted to blame someone else for manipulating him. I knew the root of this was that when I grounded him it restricted his time with Tiffani. I knew it. But at least he was taking responsibility for his decision, not putting it on anyone else. So what was the point of pushing my story over his? I reminded myself that what I wanted most was to know his mind, not to prove myself right. I had to let it go. I took a deep breath.

"It must have taken a lot of courage," I said.

"Holy shit, you have no idea. To literally break what my life had been? I had decided to do it that week. I remember sitting in the car waiting for you to get in, and I started internally talking myself out of it. You came in and I noticed you had about five printed out Edline sheets with highlighted grades. You were waving them around at me. I felt terrified starting it, really angry, but really confident and kind of powerful for the first time. It was horrible fighting with you. I don't think I had ever really seen you like that before, so mad and screaming. But I'd never felt like that towards you either.

"It sucked, but I felt great that I did it. I didn't come back to Mom's house and say, 'Oh, what have I done!' I said 'Oh shit, I did it!' I never regretted it or anything. I always felt like I made the right decision. I knew you were furious, but I knew you loved me, too. Somewhere maybe you had faith that I knew the right thing. I didn't really feel that, but subconsciously I knew you weren't going to hate me forever.

"Those first few months were a little weird being in one place. Mom didn't really avoid me, but she tried not to bring up anything about school or anything about you. She stayed sort of calm and kept her distance. I just built up again. I was doing all my homework. Teaching myself study habits, rather than having them enforced on me prepared me for college way more than any amount of rules would have. Even now, when I am planning out my week and my homework, it never feels external, like this is what I've been taught. It feels like this is what I know. This is what I need to do to please me, not somebody else.

"Maybe I was just not a typical kid. Maybe that works for every other kid and they internalize it in their own way. Maybe that's just the way I was raised and I did not have those kinds of connections or stability, and I needed to do it myself. I needed something that was stable. I needed me to be that rock, that anchor for myself. So I was this constant drifting entity trying to find my own orbit. It was terrifying and amazing for me. And then to go that next step, take massage therapy classes and decide on my own what college I wanted to go to. It was exciting that I had this idea of something I wanted to do with my life. Not something you or mom wanted me to do with my life."

Josh paused, gathering his thoughts.

"You know, in the end, Dad, you were really helpful. When I was first on my own without you, there was a certain amount of, not spite, but me thinking, I better do well now. I've been saying, 'Just let me manage my own stuff.' So now I really have to do well or it's all going to seem like bullshit. So then I just did well. It was exactly what I needed."

"Josh, I hated every day of it. I felt robbed of six months of your life. You cut me out with remarkable ruthlessness. I didn't know you possessed it. It was almost admirable. It was... a gift, actually. I can see that now. You destroyed my story of myself as a good father. That story had become a big part of my identity, my crust. It was the story of my sacrifice, my atonement, I guess. That story got me through hard times when you were small. It gave me this great sense of self-worth, because of the time I devoted to you. When you left, shit, you blew apart my tower. My friends asked me how you were, and I had to say you had gone to live full time with your mom. I felt like she won. It was painful. But I get it now. All my cherished parenting memes–protecting, structuring, guiding–they had become ineffective, worthless for you.

"So what I'm figuring out is that it's not just the memes of society that can turn you into a zombie. When you believe the story of yourself too much, that can zombiefy you too. There were times when you were 17, I remember just setting my face, rigidly determined to do it my way for your own good. So what did you do? You cut off the head of the zombie-dad."

Josh laughed.

"I get it now that the parenting part of my life is finished. I guess I'm glad it happened just the way it happened."

"Me too," said Josh, softly.

"That doesn't mean that I see everything the same way that you do."

"That's okay, Dad. I don't need to convince you that my story's more right than yours. I'm getting tired though. Should we try to get some sleep?"

"One last thing. I've been thinking as we were talking, we could not have had this conversation if you hadn't forgiven me yesterday. What you did confused me at first. How the hell could you forgive me for adultery? That's your mom's place, not yours, and I don't think she ever will. So I've learned to live without it. But I see it differently now. Going back to Rapunzel's tower, it's as if when you forgave me, you broke down some of the walls of the story that you had built around me. You let go of your grudge against me, and somehow that let me go, too."

"I sort of feel that, Dad. It's like I couldn't have talked with you about this stuff today, about my real life. I wouldn't have trusted you."

"It's a big shift. You know, until yesterday, I thought forgiveness was all about judgment and repentance and absolution. I was still inside my old Christian mythology. If somebody wronged you, they apologized, and you forgave them. It's like you are freeing them from a prison sentence. What I'm figuring out now is that the prison is in the mind of the person who holds the grudge. It's your story about them that turns them into a thing. Oh, he's a liar. She betrayed me. What an asshole. We take our prisoners and put them in our tower, walled off with our judgments."

"Dungeons."

"What?"

"We put them in the dungeons of our minds."

"Nice. So what you did yesterday, you freed me from your dungeon. It didn't matter whether or not I had personally wronged you. It was your grudge to let go of. And when you did, I felt it. I guess maybe the adultery was just the tip of the iceberg, you know for all the things that were tough between us then. I can see now that for you, I had just turned into this asshole who was trying to make you do things his way, or else. I don't know if that's accurate..."

"Oh, it's accurate," he laughed.

I continued: "I have a friend, an old guy who was a therapist I went to for a year. He's the most emotionally intelligent, empathetic man I have ever met. When he talks about his childhood though, he describes being beaten and emotionally abused almost every day. And he says, 'I am so grateful to both my parents. If not for my past, I would never have developed into the therapist I am today.' It amazed me."

"It's like you just said," said Josh, drowsily. "I'm glad it happened just the way it happened....Good night, Dad."

"Good night, Josh."

A minute later I propped myself up on an elbow: "Josh?"

"What?" he opened his eyes and looked at me. His voice sounded faintly annoyed.

"You remember I said what I was really afraid of with Tiffani was that she would get pregnant and you would be trapped? Did you ever wonder why I was so afraid of that? Does that story sound *familiar*?

"Holy Shit, Dad–it's you and Mom!"

"Exactly. It just hit me that I was transposing my story onto yours. If you married a woman like your mother and got trapped like I did, I think I would never forgive her for it."

"Never forgive who, Tiffani?"

"No, I'd never forgive–Aw, crap, god-damn!" I cursed.

I lay back down and stared up at the blue top of the tent.

"What? Dad, are you okay?"

"Ugh, I just discovered something. I meant 'never forgive your mother.' I just didn't realize how much I meant it. I never forgave your mother for turning cold on me. I say I've taken responsibility for my actions, paid my penance for my infidelity, but at the root of it, I still blame her for everything that went wrong between us. I've been keeping her in my dungeon for over twenty years. But I love my life now. I don't want it any other way. Don't you think it's time I let her go?"

"You're not going to say this to her or anything?" said Josh. I could hear the alarm in his voice. "I think she would be–'*What the hell?*'–if you said you forgave her."

Josh was right. This was exactly my first impulse. I could see it was a dumb one.

"Okay, I won't talk to her about it."

I sensed his relief. For the first time it hit me that Josh was protective of his mother, that he was a good son for her. We lay silently side by side. After a minute, I heard Josh snore.

So what is an asshole anyway? A guy who wants his own way, and will push other people around to get it. Sure, "my own way" was just making sure Josh didn't fail, for his own good. Well, I never liked hearing "for your own good" when I was a teenager. So yeah, he can forgive me for that. It would be nice though, if he could someday apologize for being an asshole right back.

The sun went down and the wind picked up. It shook the blue fabric with gale force. I imagined our tent uprooted and tumbling, us still inside it, past the outhouses and over the ledge. I tried not to think about it. I clutched my hot water bottle to my chest and shut my eyes. But sleep would not come.

We were eating lunch at a restaurant in 2007. My father was complaining to me about my sister's kids, how she needed to discipline them better.

"The way we brought you up, when you misbehaved, you got

spanked, so you knew the rules. It was Kipling's Law of the Jungle: make punishment swift and make it hurt. Then it's over and done with. It taught you self-discipline, didn't it?"

I had heard my father speak about the Law of the Jungle so many times, and said nothing, just put up the buffer. Not this time.

"Dad, you talk about Rudyard Kipling as if he were some sort of parenting guru. The Victorian Era was not the golden age of child rearing. So yeah, you thought you were teaching your children discipline. Maybe, but maybe that's not what drove me at all. But spanking did teach me to fear you. Even today, sometimes when you go to hug me, I have to brace myself so I won't flinch when you put your hands on me."

I looked into his pale blue eyes. I watched them fill with tears. He held my gaze. I could see he had taken in everything that I had said, like a boxer who had dropped his guard. What I said hit him like a fist in the face, and he took it straight.

"Tim, I had no idea...I am so, so very sorry."

That moment changed something between him and me. I felt his love in that moment, with no sentimentality, no clever barb attached. After that, I discovered I could let him hug me without feeling the urge to flinch.

Chapter Eight

Zombies On Kilimanjaro

Night 5: Barafu Camp to Uhuru Peak (5,895 meters): 5 kilometers

"Welcome tea!"

Sully called us at 11:15 p.m. We flipped on our headlamps, sat up and reached for the steaming cups as he handed them to us through the tent flaps. We sipped, still bundled in our sleeping bags, the hot mugs stinging our fingers. The air was freezing, though the wind had died to a whisper. Dozens of muffled conversations hummed in the darkness around us. I felt my heart beat fast in my chest. It felt like equal parts excitement, fear, and the physical stress of low oxygen.

"Did you sleep?" Josh asked.

"Nope. I've been lying awake for hours, thinking about what we are about to do.

"You worried?"

"Not that so much. I've been asking myself, why did people in ancient times climb mountains? Not to conquer a summit, not to plant a flag, not for a vacation. These are recent memes of modern men and women. In ancient times, most people didn't climb the peaks. They had fear of the mountain gods, they had respect. The few who did climb, they did it to receive a vision. On the mountaintop the sacred could speak in such a way that we humans could hear. Think of Moses on Mount Sinai, the Sadhus who make their pilgrimage to Mount Kailas where Shiva dwells, the Tibetan monks who meditate in Himalayan caves, Taoist sages who built their refuges in the crags of China's Holy Mountains. Climbing to high altitudes takes you away from the human-made world. It breaks you apart from the memes of everyday reality. And when you have set your mind apart, that's when you can receive a vision."

I rummaged through my bag for the little guidebook I bought about Kilimanjaro. It had a chapter on the symbolic role the mountain played in inspiring Africans' struggle for freedom. By flashlight I read a quotation spoken by Tanzania's first president, Julius Nyerere in 1959, when the land then known as Tanganyika was still under British rule:

We, the people of Tanganyika, would like to light a candle and put it on the top of Mount Kilimanjaro which would shine beyond our borders giving hope where there was despair, love where there was hate, and dignity where before there was only humiliation.

"This was a speech, Josh, calling not only for self-determination for Nyerere's country, but for all of Africa. That vision of Kilimanjaro as a beacon of independence spread across Africa. Tanganyika became one of the first self-ruling nations on the continent. Nyerere's government then offered shelter for leaders fighting colonial oppression in other parts of Africa. Sure, Africa today has its dictators, corruption, poverty and disease. But the vision of an independent Africa is nonetheless a reality.

"That glacier, Uhuru, near the peak, that Marita and Bastian were talking about, I'm reading here that *Uhuru* is the Swahili word for 'freedom.' "

"Dad, I remember before coming to Tanzania I googled 'Kilimanjaro.' It was kind of funny to see the stories that came up. So many of them were about some woman climbing to raise money for an orphanage. This guy being the first to do it in a wheelchair, to raise awareness of what disabled people could do. A baseball team doing it to help cure cancer. They weren't just climbing the mountain, they were doing it for a cause, even when the cause seemed to have nothing to do with Kilimanjaro itself."

"Yes, this is exactly what turns a project into a vision. This is all part of my work as a communications consultant, helping people create a vision that motivates people to act. A vision is a story, a commmplex, but it's not about the past. It's a story about the future. A future that can only happen if people work together to make it happen. When that vision inspires others, it can become a force that can change the world, like ending slavery, winning equal rights for women, eradicating polio. Or it can be something personal, becoming a doctor, or an artist's vision of a painting or sculpture. What is important is that the vision draws us towards making that story of the future into a reality. In a sense, we are writing humanity's next chapter before it has happened. It's the ultimate creative act."

"Dad," Josh interjected, "I hate to interrupt, but I think you are losing track of time. We better put our clothes on while you talk."

Following Marita and Bastian's advice, we started putting on every article of clothing we possessed, starting with double layers of long johns.

I continued talking as we dressed: "So to create a vision of a new future, we first need to sweep aside the old memes that hold the current reality in place. We have to create a space for change."

"Kind of what I did in leaving your house?"

"I guess that's so," I said slowly. "There's got to be some element of destruction to make way for a new creation. I think this is why climbing a mountain is much more than a symbol. Ordeal, hardship, physical exhaustion, thin air: it takes will. When we get to the top, our brains get so scrambled they can't process memes in the normal way. We can see through the cracks in our story of the world. We can let it go. We can see something else that's possible, and then take our old memes and use them to create the building blocks of a new world."

I slipped on three layers of shirts, then a fleece, Gore-tex jacket, and on my bottom half, long underwear, trousers and nylon rain pants for the wind.

"I've had my experiences, Josh, with creating a vision as a writer and running my own small business. I'm guessing you've had it too with your music and the shows you've been in–which is really a joint vision of the whole cast."

"Yeah," he said, zipping up his coat, "*Faux Show*," [a student musical Josh wrote and directed] was definitely my biggest example. I had an idea of what I wanted and had to make that from my mind. I dunno. Some force of God helped me finish it all in time. And Marta and Bastion, what they told us today about standing on the top, that climbing Kilimanjaro, they know they would make it as a couple."

"Yes, exactly! So this idea of vision is a way we can use our memes to create. Maybe for the night ahead of us, we need a vision, so that when it gets hard, it can help keep us going, all the way to the peak."

"Or we could just mindlessly stagger forward like zombies," Josh giggled.

"Right, okay," I persevered. "But this is exactly my point. If we just let our memes run the show, then we are their slaves, under their control. When we can see memes and memeplexes for what they are, and break through them from time to time, then we can use them consciously to create our future."

"I envision myself as a zombie, so, I can't die!" said Josh. "I might gnaw on your head a little bit, though Dad. *Gnnnnarwllllll*. I wonder how you say 'brains' in Swahili?"

I had to laugh. I wrapped a scarf round my neck. Josh pulled his black balaclava over his head. We each had seven layers on top and four on the bottom. Fred and Frank were waiting for us outside.

"Where are your day packs?" I asked them.

"Oh, we don't need them."

Frank took Josh's pack, heavy with water bottles, and slung it on his own back. Fred grabbed for mine, but I said I would see how far I could go with it.

The guides carried no water of their own and no food.

"No problem, we had lots to drink before we left," said Fred.

I felt a bit annoyed by Fred's casual attitude towards his own health and safety. Here Josh and I were gearing up for a major ordeal, but for them it was literally a walk in the park. "Take lots of water. Bring lots of snacks. Dress for the Arctic," they said. Now they were just going to bounce along beside us, keeping us from falling on our asses or asphyxiating in our own lung juices. On the one hand, their supreme confidence was comforting. On the other hand, it made me feel like we were soft, stupid, children, and they were our nannies. Well, in fact this was not far from the truth. We were paying them to keep us alive. It only made sense that the people best able to do this were those who could handle themselves with alacrity in high altitudes. But still it got my goat. So I was determined to hang onto my daypack as long as I could.

We marched off into the darkness. It was disorienting at first. All our time on the mountain we had been walking in daylight. We could always see the path ahead and behind, enjoying vistas that went on for miles and miles. Moving at night I had no visual sense of where I was or what kind of terrain we were covering. The small circle of my headlamp revealed only Fred's boots ahead of me on the rocky trail. I had no idea what kind of drop offs there might be as we zig-zagged blindly upward. A step to the right, a slide to the left–would it plunge us over the edge? When I looked up I could see a moving strand of luminescent white dots above us, dangling like a long strand of fireflies. These were the headlamps of other trekkers who had started the journey ahead of us.

It was cold. The night was still. The wind dropped. My seven layers soon made me sweat as we started up a steep switchback.

I unzipped and unbuttoned. Fred kept us to a slow, steady pace. It was pleasant at first just to walk with little thought for anything other than putting the next foot forward. I entered a kind of timeless zone, seeing nothing outside the glow around Fred's feet. The higher we climbed, the more effort each step required. Reaching into a pocket and tearing open a protein bar made me gasp for breath. To walk and chew at the same time was too difficult. I was getting stupider with each step.

After a few hours, I hated to look up. The headlamps on the trail in front of us always seemed impossibly high and far away. They never got any closer. Rationally I knew this was because the people who carried them were moving just like us. But the effect made it seem as if were we not gaining ground, just walking, walking, walking and yet standing still. Frank did his best to keep our spirits up. He sang in a loud and raucous voice, mixing English and Swahili. For a while he even got us to chime in with the Kilimanjaro song.

"No sleeping! No sleeping!" He hollered up the hillside to the other hikers.

Now the wind swept down from the glaciers. It jabbed into my bones like long, frozen needles. This was the penetrating cold Marita and Bastian and warned us about. I was no longer sweating. In fact, I was growing colder even as I climbed with greater exertion. I zipped all my zippers back up. I lost feeling in my right foot. I wiggled my numb toes to get some circulation back. Fred kept us marching. He never let us stop for more than a few minutes at a time. Just long enough for a sip of water. Drinking was becoming difficult. The contents of our bottles turned first to slush, then to ice, allowing little more than a frozen trickle on the throat.

Our head lamp batteries started to grow dim. We stopped to replace them, but the spares we carried in our bags had frozen and they were dead. No problem, Fred said, the light we had left would get us to the top.

"But our cameras…"

"Put some batteries inside your glove," said Fred.

I mindlessly obeyed. I took two little frigid cylinders and placed them in my palm, then pulled my glove back on.

My daypack got heavier and heavier. The five kilos were weighing me down. I surrendered the load to Fred, who shouldered it with irritating ease.

The moon came out, a crescent bowl in the sky. Beneath its faint illumination we saw Mawenza's jagged crater. Every crevice on the face of the eerie second peak stood out in strange, moonlit relief. It looked so close, I wanted to reach out a finger and touch it.

The moon also reflected off the rock face across from us on the trail. A long streak of it glowed a faint white. This was the tail of a glacier. We had reached the permanent ice. I craned my neck up to stare. But the string of lights on the trail still stretched high above us without end. I felt desperate. We stopped again to rest. Josh was suffering. He said his headache was back and pounding. Each step jarred him with pain. He asked Fred if he could take another Diamox. Fred shook his head.

"How about Advil?"

"No."

"Why not?"

"Above 5,000 meters, you can't tell what will happen. Any medicine can have unpredictable effects. It can hurt you very, very quickly. So you have to wait until we get to lower altitudes to take any pills, you understand?"

It was hard to see Josh in such pain so near to the top, but there was no arguing the point with Fred. Josh sat to rest, his back against a boulder.

"Damn it," he said. "I've got to go to the bathroom. Can I get some toilet paper?"

"Fred, is it safe? I don't want him to fall off the…"

"*Hakuna matata.* Just don't go too far," Fred said to Josh.

I watched Josh navigate his way over the rocks, hand over hand, disappearing into the blackness. I had no way of knowing whether he was okay or had dropped into the void. There would be no good way to explain it to his mother, I thought vaguely. I bit into a power bar. It broke off in brittle, frozen pieces in my mouth.

"How many times a year do you do this climb?" I asked Fred.

"Oh, about 10-15 guiding. And then a lot of us guides like to run the Uhuru Marathon."

"You're kidding me."

"Oh no, each year there's a race from bottom to the top and back. We do it in a less than a day. On the Coca-Cola trail, so it's not so far."

I felt totally demoralized. I knew Fred could do this because he was acclimatized, fit as a horse, and about 15 years younger than me. But I hated, hated to hear about anybody running to the summit when it was killing me just to keep inching towards the top.

Josh stumbled back into sight.

"*Mambo?*" asked Frank.

"*Poa kichisi, kama frickin' ndisi.* I can't believe it," he groaned. "I had to take off all those layers, and no luck!"

It was actually getting easier to walk now, because it was becoming impossible to stay focused on a single thought for very long. It felt like there was not much mental activity left inside my brain, so no resistance, no thought about how hard this was nor how much longer it would take. I knew only the sharp tingle in my frozen hands and feet, the dull ache everywhere in between, the steady heaving of my lungs and the tiny tunnel of light at my feet.

"Not far now," said Fred, checking his watch. "We have about…"

"Don't tell me the time," I cut him off with a hiss. "I don't want to know."

I longed for oblivion. I wanted no more songs. No more of Frank's amusing antics, no wisdom from Fred or demonstrations of his deftness. I didn't even care about Josh's headache. I just wanted to stay lost in the effort of pushing that next foot ahead until dawn. My mind was a black sky. The only thing that remained was the urge to keep moving.

I fleetingly remembered a film I once saw about a kind of fungus that infected grasshoppers. The fungus would attack their nervous system, slowly killing them. As it consumed them alive, it triggered the bugs' neural impulse to climb. This drove the hoppers up tall stalks of grass, and when they got to the top they would just sit still as the fungus finished them off. From this high perch, the fungus would develop its spores and release them into the air. The wind would spread the spores far and wide to infect other insects. It was a perfect transmission system, an evolutionary quirk so cunning it seemed almost evil. That's how I felt, like one of those grasshoppers dragging itself up to the top of the stalk with my last dying steps.

I had achieved the zombie vision Josh had foretold.

Eventually the stars dimmed. The sky grew soft grey. I looked out. All of Africa lay below us, covered in white mist like a smooth, ivory planet. Snow and ice layered both sides of the trail, which still twisted upwards. For the first time we could see a line of head lamps moving horizontally above us: climbers moving along on the rim of the volcano. Fred said these were the trekkers who had ascended over Mawenza's saddle to Gillman Point, following the Coca Cola route. We were close to the top.

The sky brightened into an intense pale blue as we reached the crater's rim. At last we stumbled onto level ground.

"Is this it? Are we really here?" said Josh, panting, his voice hoarse and straining. "I can't believe it. Look at it, so beautiful. This is what the whole week was for. I've just been thinking only one thing for hours, 'God, get me to the top.' "

"Me too," I gasped.

Our lungs heaved with exhilaration and exhaustion as we peered into the vast ash pit inside the extinguished core of Kilimanjaro. It stretched like a grey sea several kilometers wide, bounded by cliffs on the near side, and a rubble slope across from us that rose to a perfect inner cone streaked with ice–a volcano within a volcano. At an impossibly far distance we could see a massive glacier on the far ash shore.

At that instant the sun flashed on the horizon, a brighter sun than I had even seen. As it crested the light seemed to melt like poured gold spreading along a thin horizontal line from either side of the half-emerged orb. Light drenched the rocks, the snow, the glacier walls with a deep yellow sheen, as if the world were dipped in melted butter. The skin on our faces blazed like brass. My photos of that moment look weirdly over-exposed. Our faces appear to be shining.

Josh slumped on a rock.

"We made it, thank God we made it!" he said.

Apparently he had not yet noticed the steady stream of trekkers shuffling numbly and silently along the snowy line of the Coca-Cola trail, like a whole horde of zombies passing right in front of us and continuing along the circumference of the crater. They lurched along towards the highest point of the rim.

"Well, we can't rest here any longer, "said Fred.

"Wha–?" said Josh.

"This is only Stella Point," Fred continued. "It's not the top. It's 45 more minutes to Uhuru Peak, highest place in Africa. You take picture there with the sign. We should get going. You can't stay up here too long."

"This isn't the end?" said Josh, his voice filled with alarm.

"You have to go to the peak," said Frank. "Or no cer-ti-fi-cate!" His voice had a sing-song lilt, like he was trying to motivate a toddler.

"No certificate?" said Josh.

"Seriously," I said to Fred, "You mean if someone climbs all this way to the rim, but doesn't crawl up the last little bit they don't get a certificate?"

Fred giggled. "No way. We guides have to sign the certificate to verify you reached the top."

"Okay, this is fine!" Josh said. He was wheezing. His voice cracked like he was either crying or laughing, I couldn't tell which. "This is good enough for me, I'm content just to be here, just totally content, ha ha ha." He started coughing.

I struggled to my feet. Fred gave Josh a hand, and he staggered up too. We stepped back onto the path with all the other trekkers and started walking once more, as if carried forward by the collective momentum. The path alternated between gravel and frozen ridges of snow, with shards of ice sticking up with sharp, serrated edges as long as daggers. Stepping over them was near impossible. These were penitentes, the name given to the blades of ice formed when new snow starts to melt on high mountain peaks. It was like walking over a field of giant shark teeth. Here and there the ice had been worn into a path by the heavy foot traffic, but in other places we had to pick our way carefully through it so as not to trip and hurt ourselves.

I noticed people walked in both directions now, some shuffling up towards the peak, some already on their way back down. I pushed forward hoping to generate enough energy for this last surge through the ice. My brain dissolved into obscenities. I really didn't know what I was thinking. I just moved forward, muttering to myself. I wasn't even noticing whether or not the others were following. So I did not notice when behind me, Josh fell.

He told later how it happened:

"I got up to follow you. My only thought was to keep going. There was a fork in the trail and I didn't choose a path. It threw me off. I was so exhausted I just dropped down in the middle. I lay on the hard, sharp snow. I thought maybe I would stop here and relax. Maybe I didn't really need a certificate. I was okay, just lying here on the ground, no problem. Quite nice here. Sooo much more comfortable than walking. I thought maybe I would just close my eyes for a bit.

"Then I remembered Marita. I was really proud of her, enduring nausea, vomiting on the climb, just sucking it up and keeping on going. She was really strong. I opened my eyes and saw this pair of old ladies passing me on the trail. 'I can make it,' I told myself.

"Next thing I knew, Frank was at my side, trying to pull me back to my feet. Sort of vaguely through a cloud I heard Fred say to him, 'Is he okay? Maybe we should be careful with him?' "

"That snapped me back to myself. I realized they were discussing whether or not they should take me back down. I said to myself, 'Fuck no! I'm 15 minutes from the top.' "

"Somehow I got myself up and pushed ahead. Frank was grabbing at my arm. Were they going to hold me back? I just started putting one foot in front of the other. I knew I had to keep moving to show them I was okay. My head was killing me but I was still feeling so good at the same time."

When I looked back at Josh on the trail, I just saw Frank with his hand clamped on Josh's elbow, the way a nurse might hold an elderly patient's arm when taking him out for a stroll.

"Frank was driving me nuts," Josh recounted. "I know he was worried I was going to fall again. But he wouldn't let go of me. So when the path narrowed and I had to walk in front of him, he was actually pulling me backward and down, making it harder for me. I was getting hot walking in the sun, so I would unzip my coat and stuff. But every time I would stop for a breath, Frank would start zipping me up again, wrap my scarf tight around my throat, like a mom with a kid. I wanted to tell him to fuck off and leave me alone. But then I got scared he might force me to go back down the mountain.

"I just remember seeing the looks on everyone's faces. All the people going up looked like sluggish, brainless, sunken monsters. The ones coming down seemed so happy and invigorated. Whatever transformation happened at the peak, I wanted that and nothing else."

I marched on ahead, driven towards the summit, oblivious of Josh and what he was going through. Uhuru Glacier came into view to the south of the rim. For days we had stared up at this gigantic white mass as it towered above us. Now to look at it at eye level, this vast, hundred-foot high crust of ice wrapped around the outer edge of the crater, I felt exhilarated, awed. You could see how it had slid off the rim, leaving a flat field of snow and ice shards behind. It reminded me of a geological ice cream cone that had started to melt. I got out my camera, popped in my hand-warmed batteries, and started taking pictures.

Josh caught up to me and we walked together up the final rocky slope. Suddenly, after eight hours of climbing, we reached the end of the trail. It was marked by a big wooden sign:

Congratulations! You are now at Uhuru Peak, Tanzania, 5895 M.
AMSL*
(Above Mean Sea Level)
Africa's Highest Point
World's Highest Freestanding Mountain

Trekkers from various countries queued up to pose and have their pictures taken by their guides. Everybody had shaken off their stupor. They laughed and beamed broad smiles, arms slung around their comrades' shoulders, and thumbs up. I caught snippets of French, Japanese, Russian, Korean, Brazilian Portuguese, Dutch. It was like a mini UN summit. Josh and I dutifully waited our turn. We grinned for the camera, then stumbled over to a pile of rocks to sit and catch our breath.

From here we had a panoramic view. To the north, in front of us, we could see almost all the way round the inside rim of the crater. The sun glinted off the vast sea of ash and turned it to silver. We could see inside the snow-covered inner cone. Its core was a perfectly round dark hole. It looked like God had dropped a powdered donut and left it there. Behind the cone, further east, we could see the top edge of the northern ice fields, the largest ice mass left on the mountain. Somewhere over there was the station of the American climate research teams. To the west outside the crater we could see Mawenzi, its hump of jagged teeth jutting through the grey mists below. Just behind us, past the sign we could see the very top of Uhuru Glacier, where its white back just started curving down over the outside of the rim. This was the tip of the glacier we had looked up at after ascending Barranco Wall two days ago.

Josh smiled a woozy smile.

"Every pain sensor in my body is firing," he said. "But all I feel is happy. I've never been in so much pain and felt so much joy at the same time in my life. Thank God I don't have to walk up any more! There is no more up! There's only *down* from here!"

I felt a wave of pride. I slapped him on the back and offered him a frozen chocolate protein bar. We gnawed off small fragments.

Josh shot a short video of us at the peak. It's hilarious and excruciatingly painful to watch. Though I wasn't suffering physical discomfort, it's obvious in the video that delirium has hit me hard. All my normal self-moderating controls have been shut down, so that in this moment of victory I sound like a complete moron. I sound like Steve Cartell's clueless and obnoxious character from the TV sit-com *The Office*:

Josh: "We're on the top. We did it. There's the sign…Let me get the full…glacier."

Josh's nose sounds stuffed. He's sniffing. Is the low pressure blowing out our sinuses? He hands the camera to me, the scene wobbles precariously. I pan to Josh:

Tim: "There's the man!" I enthuse in this weird, pitchy, gravelly voice, "On top of Kilimanjaro! Joshua! The Survivor!"

At first Josh is smiling back at the camera. But soon he's looking sheepish and shaking his head as I rant. The fungus has eaten my brains, and there's nothing left but manic-daddy memes. I hand him back the camera, and he zooms in on me. I break into song, the chorus of the singer Juluka's famous tune about Kilimanjaro. It's suddenly a scene from a demented African version of *The Sound of Music*. I sing:

I'm sittin' on top of Kilimanjaro
I can see a new tomorrow
I'm sittin' on top of Kilimanjaro
I cast away all my sorrows

I know what I was aiming for. It's a song about vision. But I come across like Pee Wee Herman on cocaine.

Josh is getting delirious too. He's got it into his head that he can get all the other trekkers to do a group cheer for his video.

"Hey everybody, who wants to help me with something?" he yells with the camera rolling.

Nobody even looks at him.

"We'll all shout something all at once!"

A few are looking around now, as if they are thinking, "What's wrong with this guy?"

"We'll all do something really quick! Repeat after–Hey! Come on, everybody!"

There's a pause.

"Nobody? Okay…You guys all suck!" Josh flips the camera off, then back on again:

"Oh yeah, one more thing," he hollers loudly: "*Poa kichisi, kama ndisi!* Owwwooooooooooo!"

The wolf howl is a nice touch. Everyone in the video is ignoring him totally. In the final frame, he pans quickly back to himself and sticks his tongue out at the camera.

Chapter Nine

Down

Day Six: Uhuru Peak to Mweka Camp (3,068 meters) 12 kilometers

"Okay, my brothers! Time to go down," said Fred.

I suppose he had seen enough of our freakish behavior. It must have been an indicator to him that our brains were on the verge of exploding with fluid.

"You're the boss, Fred, you're the boss!" I called out loudly.

Frank grabbed Josh by the arm and started leading him back along the volcano's rim. I hung back. I wanted to take a few more pictures before we left. Fred urged me again to keep moving.

"You're the boss! You go ahead, I'll catch up," I waved him on.

He eyed me suspiciously, then turned and walked after Frank and Josh.

Everything at the top was so crisp and clear. I didn't want to leave this dazzling African freezer in the sky. I took photo after photo of the crater walls, the glaciers, the ash pit. From where I stood, I could see the glacier inside the crater that I had glimpsed from Stella Point. From this perspective, however, I could see that it was not in fact massive and far away, but much closer and actually rather puny. It looked to be only 5 meters (15 feet) high. Looking closely, I could see how it had split down the middle, with parts broken off forming little ice islands. I realized this must be Furtwängler Glacier, the one I had read about in the *Nature* article. This was the glacier the researchers measured which had shrunk fifty percent in the last decade. They said it was waterlogged and would vanish completely in the next several years. Looking down on Furtwängler, I could imagine it shriveling into a mound of slush, and then a great puddle that would be swiftly lapped up by the dry air. After many thousands of years, this great white creature was dying swiftly.

My hands and feet were getting numb from standing still. I aimed at Furtwängler for one final shot. The camera slipped from my frozen fingers and dropped onto the penitentes at my feet. A spear of ice hit the side of the lens, kinking the zoom so that it would no longer retract or take pictures. I punched buttons with no response. I know, I said to myself, I need to bash it with a rock. If I pound the lens at the right angle I can unkink it. I got down on my knees to look around but fortunately there were no rocks where I was standing, only ice and gravel. Oh well, I said cheerfully to myself, pocketing the broken camera. As I stood back up, I got dizzy. My sense of balance was off. It was as if I had vertigo. I staggered back a step. I was right on the edge of the rim. A jolt of adrenaline brought me back to my senses. What the hell was I doing all alone? How long have I been here? I turned and walked swiftly and stiffly back down along the rim.

Now that I was on my way down, I felt great, energized even, despite the physical exhaustion that forced me to move slowly. I was so happy to be alive! So many people were still making their way up, a long queue of faces and complexions, young and old, thin and chubby, white, black, oriental. The whole world was walking to the roof of Africa. They looked tired, spent. Many were gasping and being helped along by their Tanzanian guides. I felt a pang of empathy for all of them.

"You're almost there!" I called out encouragingly to each one as I bounced past. "You can make it! Not far now!"

They looked up at me skeptically, scornfully, with withering glances.

"Oh my God, Dad," said Josh when I caught up to him and the guides at Stella Point and told him about these interactions. "You're that annoyingly cheerful guy everyone hates! You know, this is really not fair," he said with a laugh. "Why do I get the headache and you get the euphoria?"

He was so adorable, whatever it was he was talking about.

Fred handed us our walking poles. I said I didn't need them, but he sternly insisted.

"You're the boss, Fred, you're the boss!" I chortled merrily.

Descending the nearly vertical part of the outer rim was hard. My legs shook all the way, just from holding back the momentum of my body. Going up, if you fall, you can catch yourself easily. On the way down, a misstep can lead to a tumble. As we passed the last of the snow and ice, the slope leveled off a bit and we got our first glimpse of the terrain below. It was a bad joke. I wanted to punch someone. All night while climbing I had been terrified that a gust of wind or a misplaced step might hurtle one of us into the abyss. But the vista at our feet was nothing more than a broad gravel slope, no more treacherous than a beginners ski hill. Here and there the trail wound in and around boulders, but it was not in the least bit dangerous. There was no way either of us could have fallen off or hurt ourselves unless we'd tripped and landed on our faces.

A worse sight was passing those poor trekkers still on their way up. Not just the elderly and the portly, but even fit, young climbers who had obviously been whacked by AMS. They were suffering, and sweating too, now that the sun was getting high and hot. One heavyset white woman in a pink parka had two guides with her. One walked backwards in front of her, pulling her arms. The other walked behind, pushing her backside. She was moving very slowly. Others trekkers sat with their heads in their hands, their guides pensive at their sides. How do you tell someone who has been on the mountain for a week and climbing all night that they are not going to make it, that they must turn around and start the long, joyless stumble all the way down?

After we had descended for another hour, Fred and Frank directed us left onto a different path than the one we had climbed. Instead of rocks and boulders, this part of the mountainside was covered with scree. Frank explained that the fastest and easiest way down was to jump into the loose rubble and let it carry you down using the poles like a skier.

I hadn't skied in three decades, but I felt totally confident in my ability. I pushed off, jumping out into space, falling and planting my feet in the scree. I felt the loose rubble give way beneath my feet, just like skiing in powder snow. I leapt again, planting my poles, swiveling, turning, running a few steps and then jumping again. From a state of near total exhaustion, now I was filled with the thrill of the velocity of the controlled fall, dust and pebbles flying in my wake. I felt like a kid. It was all I could do not to yell Yipeeee! I paused for a breather to see Frank scrambling behind me, madly trying to keep up, calling after me. Josh and Fred were way behind, still much higher up. I had slid down far and fast.

Josh was walking like an old man, taking small, doddering steps, stopping to rest every few minutes. I watched and waited a few momently, impatiently.

I wanted to call up to him: "Come on! Take a leap! You can fly!"

I realized his headache was probably getting worse. God, I was just lucky I didn't have any altitude symptoms. I hung out on a rock till Frank got close, then I leaped out again, hit the gravel and flew down the hill, yelping quietly to myself, slaloming along, whoosh, whoosh. I'm ready for the Olympic Sand Skiing Championships, I chuckled to myself. I looked back up the hill and groaned with exasperation. Ugh, I have to wait for Josh again. Damn, I wish he would hurry up. I feel like I'm the kid now and he's the grandfather. Next thing I know he'll be calling down at me, "You watch out there, sonny! You're going too fast! You don't know what you're doing! It's too dangerous! You'll twist your ankle! Break your leg!"

"Yah!" I jeered back at him in my mind, "You're not the boss of me now!" Leap, whoosh, whoosh, skid, skid! "I can fly over the rocks. I–"

Then it hit me: Oh shit, this is insane! This is total euphoria-induced recklessness. No wonder Frank's chasing after me. I'm out of control. I'm just one bad landing or one buried rock away from a helicopter ride home. I forced myself to wait for the others to catch up. Josh gave me a withering look but said nothing. His face was grey. Together we sipped the last bits of our water, which had finally thawed out again. I had kicked up a lot of dust, and we were coughing, though it was just as likely pulmonary AMS. Our lungs had probably strained past their point of endurance.

After two more hours the slope leveled out into a broad valley, likely the retreating path of a long-gone glacier. Our water was finished and our throats were parched. Coughing felt raw and painful. Fred and Frank had refused to share any of our supplies. I couldn't imagine how they were still smiling. Josh said his head was still pounding, even as we descended. I could tell he was putting his last effort into this final mile back to camp. My euphoria fizzled out. All I felt now was wrung-out dead.

We had been walking for eleven hours when we got back to camp. Sully greeted us with a loud *Jambo!* and a big, heartfelt hug. He seemed genuinely proud of us, and assured Josh that his headache would be better soon.

Our bodies were slick with old sweat and dust as we stripped off our many layers. It was like peeling a pair of rotten, slimy onions. We scrubbed down with man wipes and dressed in clean clothes. Soon we were sitting in the familiar comfort of our dining tent, waiting for Sully to welcome lunch.

"Dad, this was the physically toughest thing I've ever done in my life," said Josh. "Chunks of it were okay, but the altitude sickness, the darkness, I don't know how I kept going. I really did feel like a zombie."

"Me too. You gave us a vision and it became our reality. Thanks a lot."

He told me then about his fall at the top. I was mortified. What kind of a father...

"I was just wasted, in so much pain," he said. "I was hoping for some of that euphoria you were talking about! You sure got it good. You were like 'Oh, it's all so beautiful!' And then on the way down you were saying 'hi' to everyone: 'Hi, my name's Tim, I'm from Canada!' "

"I was saying this?"

"Yeah. Then all that jumping on the skree slope ! You acted like a maniac. I was really worried about you. I was going to say, 'Dad, be careful!' You looked like a little kid, throwing yourself into it without thinking. Every time I would get close you would jump off again."

"So now you know a bit of what it's like to be a parent."

He laughed.

"You know," said Josh, suddenly reflective, "you have to respect the Tanzania government for having the summit certificate. They could make it easier for people. They could put in a cable car or heck, even a road up that slope. But they don't. The mountain's difficultness is allowed to remain part of the experience. It's kind of amazing that this is one place on earth you can only reach by foot. So it means something that we have to do it on our own legs and lungs."

We ate lunch hungrily, emptying the pot of cream of mushroom soup. Instead of crackers, the dish was garnished with a plate of chocolate biscuits.

Fred slipped in through the tent. We cheered and applauded, feeling so grateful for his guiding abilities that got us to the top. He accepted our applause with a wide grin. But he also had some bad news to share. Josh's "Headache Brother"–the Dane we had passed on our walk from Lava Tower to Barranco–had had to abandon his climb last night due to AMS.

"Okay, you have 90 minutes rest, then it's a three-hour walk to tonight's campsite," Fred told us.

"You're joking, right?" said Josh.

"Seven kilometers. Don't worry, brothers! *Hakuna matata*, it is all downhill."

Fred giggled and waved goodbye as he left the tent. He wasn't kidding. I suddenly remembered Marita and Bastian telling us they had to move on in the afternoon after their climb.

Outside our tent we ran into Mike the Canadian and Bryce the Australian. We hadn't seen them since day one on the mountain. They told us their group was climbing the summit that evening. We gave them our advice, just as Marita and Bastian had briefed us the day before. We knew it couldn't possibly prepare them for what they were about to endure. They wanted to talk more, but we were about to collapse. We wished them luck, then crawled into our tent for an all-too-short nap. This time I slept.

The route to Mweka Camp was a steady descent across a blasted landscape strewn with boulders. White "everlastings" reappeared in the barren rock fields, then scrubby bushes, then conifers. After five days walking above the clouds, we now entered the tops of them. Closed in by the fog, it felt like a solitary walk. Most of the porters had headed down early in the morning and we met few other trekkers on the trail. My feet hurt and I had to stop and apply moleskin. My scree-skiing adventure had caused the leather interior of my boots to bunch up around the front of my feet, rubbing painfully against the tender places on my toes, which were now swollen.

Josh got on a jag about multiplayer online games that allowed interaction with other people who could be sitting at computer terminals all across the world. I once sat with Josh as he played *Team Fortress*, dazzled not just by the speed, violence, and cartoon humor of the game, but also by the incredible coordination required of the team players. I wondered how this reliance on high-adrenaline visual stimulation without a real physical counterpart will affect the next generation's ability to envision and create their own future, rather than just passively digest the entertaining memes streamed into their brains.

We took a break under some bushes. Bushes? I hadn't seen such normal vegetation in five days. We drank water and I pulled off my socks to apply new moleskin. The cool air felt good on my sweaty feet. I felt the sudden need to push back against the videogame meme virus that had so thoroughly infected Josh. We got up and started walking again. The path was now laid with flat stones. Where it dropped, it was tiered with steps.

"Let me ask you a question, Josh. What would you say is the difference between your experience at home, lying on a couch playing a video game, and here on Kilimanjaro?"

Josh walked in silence awhile. "Well, there's a weightiness, a heaviness. Because, I dunno, it's real. When you look up at Kilimanjaro, there's a sort of 'Oh, Wow!' experience. There's an awe of the mountain. But with man-made things there's, well, not awe, but maybe an excitement in that we're just as thrilled to see something new or wonderful, like an iPod Touch with all the applications and everything. You go 'Wow! That's really cool!' But it's a different sense of wonder than a mountain, you know? A natural wonder as opposed to a man-made one."

"I think what you've hit on, Josh, is that the awe we experience in front of a mountain like Kilimanjaro gives us a sense of connection with something much bigger than us. I think we need this sense of awe in our lives, at least I know I do. It's why we want to stare at a mountain, a rainbow, the ocean, a sunset, or look up for hours at the night sky, as opposed to just going 'Eh,' and moving on. That's why, I guess, 40,000 people a year pay to walk to the top of Kilimanjaro."

"Maybe," said Josh, skeptically. "But it could just as well be that in the world we're accustomed to, we're just not used to this kind of awe. For somebody who lives on a mountain, maybe Kilimanjaro is not the greatest thing ever, just 'Eh, there's the glacier.' "

"Let's ask Fred," I said. "Hey, Fred," I called out, as he was walking well ahead of us, "Do you ever get bored of climbing up Kilimanjaro?"

He laughed and called back over his shoulder, "You are crazy!"

"But isn't there a kind of man-made wonder that evokes the same sense of awe?" Josh argued. "Those churches, like that one we saw when we went to London, what was it, Saint Paul's? You just kind of go, 'How was that even built? It's so huge!' It almost seems like a natural wonder."

"Perhaps, but the scale is so different. Take the most massive human building ever made, the Great Pyramid of Giza. You would need about four thousand of them, stacked all together, to build something the size of Kilimanjaro."

"Really? You calculated that?"

"Well, yeah, as a matter of fact I did. It's an underestimation." Josh shook his head.

"But look at the porters with their loads," he persisted. "You think they experience awe of the mountain on this trek? You want the porters to experience awe, plug them into *Team Fortress* for an hour."

"Okay, so maybe there you have a point. I guess I agree the human brain can take any wonder and turn it into wallpaper. The point I'm trying to make, though, is that something gets lost when we stop feeling the sense of awe we get from the vastness of nature. This is one of the reasons I took you into the wilderness when you were a kid. To me there is just a fundamental difference between the world of our memes and the world outside of our memes. Our memes have not only helped us physically reshape the natural world, they have also mentally reshaped how we perceive it. One of my favorite philosophers, Martin Heidegger, wrote a brilliant essay about 60 years ago called *The Question Concerning Technology*, in which he asked how modern technology shapes our way of looking at the world. He wrote that our technology frames the world as a 'standing reserve' which we perceive as existing for our purposes. For example, when you build a hydroelectric dam, you change a river into a reservoir that exists as stored potential energy to power the turbines. So in a sense, the world of nature as it exists in itself becomes hidden from us.

"My most vivid personal experience of this came one summer in my early twenties when I was working at a hotel in the Yukon, right on the Arctic Circle. One morning I saw one of the guests standing outside at the back of the hotel looking at the vast tundra surrounding us. You could see for 100 kilometers in every direction without spotting another building, just the thin ribbon of road. The guy had silver hair and paunch. He struck me as a business man on vacation. I was thrilled to see him just soaking in this wild expanse. I came over and stood next to him, just to enjoy the moment. 'What a waste,' he said, more to himself than to me. He shook his head slowly. 'You'd think they could do something with all this empty real estate.' "

"Wow," said Josh.

"Yeah, it made me feel profoundly sad. Heidegger then asks the question: What happens to us when our technology conceals nature? I would rephrase it like this: What happens when we totally surround ourselves with our memes? Everything we see becomes a reflection of the contents of our minds. It's as if we have turned the world into a house of mirrors, reflections hitting reflections. This is what happens when we walk into a shopping mall or office building, or even a golf course.

"Computer games, they take this to meta-level. We can interact with images of our friends on the screen, or enter into virtual worlds like *The Sims, Second Life, Team Fortress*, and the whole experience is manufactured. It's 100% memes, with nature totally concealed. Don't get me wrong, I don't think there's any more harm in playing videogames than engaging in any other memes. But I can see how easy it can be to just be consumed by them.

"This is not just about butterfly watching and tree hugging. There are consequences when we can't perceive the world outside our memes. For the most part, people are unaware of how humans chew up nature to make consumer goods. We have no idea that eating hamburgers creates deforestation in the Amazon. Or that a teak bookshelf for sale at a discount furniture store came from trees illegally logged in Burma. To help deal with these problems, a lot of environmental organizations, especially WWF, the one I work with as a consultant, have gotten really smart at creating 'sustainable supply chains.' This means tracing and certifying the natural materials that go into products to make sure they are grown, mined or harvested in ways that are not destructive. If people think about where their stuff comes from and boycott destructive products, this can do a lot to preserve the wild nature we humans also depend on for our water and our food. The environmental narrative of nature as something that needs to be preserved from industrialization is actually a very new mythos, certainly less than 100 years old. It's only a small minority of people on the planet who actually get this story in a way that changes their behavior."

Josh had remained silent while I spoke. I realized my reflection had turned into a rant.

"So, any response?" I asked.

"I dunno. It's depressing. I feel like you're telling me this like you want me to, I don't know, sign up and change the world."

"Hmmm...I guess I'm still an evangelical at heart."

We both gave the feeblest of laughs.

We were back in the cloud forest now. The trees grew taller and the vegetation got lusher with every step we took down the mountain. The air felt thick and moist. Clouds hovered above our heads. As we walked into the final campsite, we saw that the ground was covered with bright green grass. It was disorienting.

Josh and I looked at our little blue tent, set up on what looked like a lawn. We exchanged a quick glance. We were both totally spent. We had been walking for fifteen of the past seventeen hours.

Sully had our bowls of hot water ready for us.

"Welcome tea!"

Sully had switched his woolen winter cap for one of faux leopard fur. Funny that he was still wearing a hat in the warmer weather.

"Friend, Josh! Josh-Papa!" he touched Josh's arm and dipped out of the tent.

"I wish I could take him home with me," said Josh.

"You would look mighty strange as the only sophomore in university with your personal waiter."

We took our seats in the folding blue chairs before the blue tablecloth and waited by candlelight as he brought us our last supper.

"Welcome, Rice and Tuna Stew!"

We ate hungrily. Despite our appetites, Josh and I agreed it was going to be a long time before I wanted tuna anything again.

When Sully returned with avocado and orange for our dessert, we asked about his family. He told us in halting English that he had a son, Rama–short for Ramadan–and a daughter Fatoosh.

"You have email so we can write?" asked Josh

"Sure!" he nodded, giving us that beautiful smile. "Friend Josh!"

It hit me when he left the tent:

"Sully," I said to Josh. "I thought his name was Solomon. But Sully's kids have Muslim names. He isn't Solomon. 'Sully' is short for 'Suleiman.' "

"It's the same name, isn't it?"

"Yeah, I guess you're right. Suleiman, Solomon. Same name, different religion."

Night fell. Animal noises croaked and trilled in the jungle over the tumbling hum of human voices. I could fell the wet, oxygen-rich air filling my lungs like an intoxicant, putting me to sleep. I struggled to stay awake as Josh and I talked about the amazing twenty-four hours we had just shared.

"I know why they call it a 'once in a lifetime experience'" said Josh. "I'm so glad we did it. But once is enough."

My father turned eighty in 2010. He wears a hearing aid and has diabetes, with the associated loss of feeling in his fingers and toes. But he still plays golf, and both he and my mother remain mentally sharp. A few months after the trip up Kilimanjaro, he and I spoke on the phone. The conversation turned to how my twelve-year old nephew was dealing with a kid at school who was bullying him. Luc had signed up for a martial arts class, which I said showed better strategic sense than my father or I ever had.

"When you run into a bully, you just need to mark him, bloody his lip, then he will leave you alone" said my father. "You remember the advice I gave you when you were in school that helped you..."

"No, it didn't help," I said bluntly. "There were five of them. They pinned my arms and jumped on me. Your advice didn't help. It just made me feel ashamed so I didn't talk about it to you any more."

He went silent.

"I'm sorry, Tim," he said at last. "I meant it to help. I guess I didn't really understand what you were going through."

He had dropped his guard and again became the vulnerable man that I loved. It felt good when I told him what really happened to me. But this time, I wanted more than just the satisfaction of smashing his story. I wanted to know, who was he, really?

"Were you bullied as a kid?" I asked.

"Boxing was mandatory at the school boarding school where I was sent after my dad was killed. Because I was so heavy, I ended up in a weight class facing a kid who was two years older than me. That thug beat me bloody. The second year, the same kid beat me again. By the third year, I learned to fight, and I beat him so badly that in my forth

year no one in the school would get in the ring with me."

I had heard this Hemingway version of his boxing days before. It wasn't what I wanted.

"What was it like for you to be bullied?"

He told me then what it was like to be a fat kid in a school full of boys, many who had also lost their fathers in the war. For the first time I got this picture of a place full of trauma, pain and isolation, devoid of compassion. He told me that he kept a journal through those miserable years. In it he recorded specifically the things he endured and how he taught himself to survive.

"You never told me about this journal," I said, astonished. "Do you still have it? I'd love to read it."

"No, it's gone. I never told anyone about it before."

"Why did you write it?"

"I did it so that when I was a father, I could better understand my kids, and maybe help them so they would never have to go through what I went through. I guess you could say becoming a good father became a lifelong obsession for me."

Suddenly I understood. Abandoned in this awful school by his dead father and neglectful, distressed mother, my father had turned his suffering into something that might be of use to his own unborn children. He coped with his loss by creating a vision of his future family, with children he could love and understand and never abandon, no matter what. It was an act of hope and courage.

"Were you trying to be like your dad?"

He sighed.

"My dad died when I was still young. I know I idealized him."

"Well, Dad, I guess you did your kids the favor of living long enough so we could get over our idealization. You know, I spent a lot of time as a young man pushing back against you, trying to make myself different from you. In the process, in some ways I've become a lot like you. I guess it's taken me till my fifties to accept that, and maybe even be a bit grateful for it."

At the heart of his story of the journal I discovered that my father had passed on to me an important meme. Twenty years ago I when I made the decision to move to Washington to be with Josh, I knew with a deep congruence that I could never abandon my son. That was the start of my story, trying to become a good father, the story which defined my life for 17 years.

Chapter Ten

Still Itself

Day Seven: Mweka Camp to Mweka Gate (1,640m)
10 kilometers

Birds sang at dawn, waking me. I had unzipped my sleeping bag during the night and thrown off the top layer. Wearing only my undershorts, I still felt comfortably warm in the tent. Through the blue fabric, I saw dew drops beaded on the tent's surface. I could hardly believe how the climate had changed in a single day. Just 24 hours ago we were walking on ice. Suddenly I remembered that I had broken my camera. I pulled it out of my day bag and put in fresh batteries. I grasped the kinked zoom lens firmly and applied pressure. It clicked straight. The camera whirred and the lens retracted, as good as new. I smiled, recalling how trying to smash the lens with a rock had seemed such a reasonable approach on the summit. I clicked through my photos and looked at Furtwängler Glacier. It seemed so tiny.

As I had said to Josh at the beginning of our trek, human-sized brains evolved to solve human-sized problems. Climate Change is too big and too slow for us to notice easily. As a result, the human race is the proverbial frog in the cooking pot. Turn up the temperature gradually and we will just float around happily until we are boiled. We are already seeing Climate Change all around us. In North America in the past few years we've experienced the worst droughts and floods on record in the Midwest, while hurricanes and tornadoes are increasing in frequency and force in the south, killing hundreds. In the north, beetles have destroyed vast pine forests in Montana and British Columbia because the winters are no longer cold enough to destroy the pests. It's worse in Africa where severe droughts cause famine, and in Asia where ever-increasing floods from the Indus, Ganges, Brahmaputra, Yangzi, and Mekong have drowned thousands, left millions destitute, and shattered the economies of some of the poorest people on the planet.

It's not that we can't connect the dots. The problem is that we have not yet organized the facts of Climate Change into a new mythos. Many scientists are now referring to the modern industrial era as the beginning of a new geologic period, *The Anthropocene*, which recognizes humanity's significant impact on the planet. What's unique about this new era is we have a choice in determining whether the earth's climate will remain stable, or will become chaotic and lead to mass extinctions and the collapse of civilization. But this new definition has not yet turned into our story. So the facts just bounce off.

Me too, I realized. The car that I drive, the home that I heat and air-condition, my plane ticket to Africa: what difference is there between me and that Evangelical Congressman who believes God won't let Climate Change happen? I recalled Hemingway's book, *The Snows of Kilimanjaro*. It's the story of a writer dying of gangrene in savannah beneath the shadow of Kilimanjaro. He regrets wasting his life writing stories about rich, vain and frivolous people. That would be us. That would be our story.

What will be the narrative my "Baby Boom" generation will tell to Josh's generation as we hand the world over to them in the next twenty years? Will we say: "Sorry we couldn't fund solar and wind power because we spent trillions of dollars on unnecessary wars and bailing out banks that lent recklessly. Sorry we couldn't mandate replacing gas guzzlers with electric cars when we had the technology, because we didn't want to impede economic growth during a recession. Sorry we couldn't reach a global agreement to stop burning coal, because Americans didn't want the Chinese to get ahead of them. Sorry we stripped the forests bare, drained the wetlands dry, and emptied the seas of edible fish. Sorry about the earth's ecological systems collapsing. Sorry we thought only of ourselves, and not of you. Our neglect is your inheritance."

"Welcome breakfast," Sully's voice called through the tent flaps, breaking my thoughts.

Sully served our last bowl of millet porridge and crepes. As we ate, I told Josh about my morning meditation on Furtwängler Glacier.

"I don't want to be sorry about the state of the world your generation will inherit, Josh. But the fact is, if my generation doesn't act on Climate Change soon, your generation will be screwed. Our mythos has kept us focused on the wrong threats. First the Afghan, then the Iraq war. Then the US alone spent three trillion dollars during the 2009 economic crisis to boost the economy and bail out the banks. Now the politicians say there's no money to prevent Climate Change and God forbid we tax carbon emissions in a downturn! But if our ecological systems collapse, there's not going to be a bailout, because there's no extra planet we can borrow from to bail us out with more food and water."

Josh chewed his pancake quietly for a while, then said, "Well, maybe like the Doomsday Clock during the Cold War, we need a giant Global Warming Thermometer to remind us what's happening."

"That, Josh, would be an excellent meme. Or maybe a humongous melting popsicle?"

"Like Kilimanjaro itself?"

"Exactly. Wouldn't it be cool if people rallied around the idea of turning back Climate Change before the glaciers vanish on Kilimanjaro? Forty thousand people come to Kilimanjaro each year. I bet most of them don't even know the story the mountain has to tell us. Maybe the researchers who work on the ice fields could do something to get the word out, like put up a plaque on

Uhuru Peak explaining how the glaciers are melting..."

"Yeah, then when people show their photographs of Kilimanjaro they can pass that story on, too. They can text it, twitter it, post it, write songs, stories, even plays, books, and videogames, send out all kinds of new memes."

"Maybe this is the real task that joins your generation and mine, Josh: creating a new mythos, one that will give us a vision of how humankind can live in harmony with nature, and pull us back from the edge of destruction."

After breakfast the porters all lined up for photographs. They sang a Swahili song for us, part of an end-of-trek tradition for all tourists. From camp it was a three-hour walk to the park gates. The path here was broad and straight through the jungle, well-tended, with smooth edges. It felt soft on the feet after so much rock. In places it was muddy and slippery beneath our well-worn boots. The soil turned deep red in color.

Fred seemed lighthearted as we struck out. He told us it would be two weeks before his next guiding job. Guides often worked only half the time even in high season because there was a surplus of them, and the companies tried to share out the work equally among them.

"So what will you do after this trip?

"I thought I would go see my sister in Tanga, so I can visit my son."

"Fred, that makes me so happy," I said.

"You made me think about spending more time with Colin," Fred told me with a smile.

He then fell back with other guides and we lost track of him. Doubtless they were regaling each other with tales of the foibles and quirks of their clients.

"I suppose this is what the Coca Cola Trail is like," Josh said to me. "I liked our path better, all narrow and rough, with no huts to sleep in on the way."

"Me too. I'm surprised how the park authorities have done so much to keep the place as natural as possible, just a few ranger outposts and outhouses. I mean, this was probably not due to some great plan. It's not like it would be easy to install a cable car or build a restaurant on the summit. But it's easy to imagine spoiling the wildness of the mountain. Instead, it's still…"

"Still itself."

"Yeah."

"Dad, I'm glad it was so hard to make it to the summit. It meant something that we had to work for it. I've never been so exhausted in my life. Climbing, you respected the mountain."

"I know. My knees still ache."

"Mine too."

"Dad, I'm so grateful. Thanks."

We walked awhile in silence, enjoying the warm air and the spongy softness of the ground beneath our feet.

"I'm grateful too Josh. Not just for the climb. You share a life with your kid for so long, you think you are both living the same narrative. It was great for me to hear you tell your story. As we've been walking this mountain I've thought so much about father-son relationships, how the memes get passed on–or not. Not just ours. I've also been thinking about my relationship with my father, how much energy I spent pushing back against him. At times he seemed such a domineering force, pressuring me to be what he wanted me to be. But that actually helped me become my own independent person. When it came to raising you, I wanted to raise you differently. I wanted to just let you be you, not control you or push you. But from listening to your story, I guess I did come off as domineering at times…"

"You think?" Josh interrupted with a laugh.

"But it turns out that you pushing back against me helped get you started on your own path to independence. I guess I'm surprised to discover I've got reason to be grateful for what I disliked most about my father. It makes me feel sad I've still got this buffer against him after all these years. I guess he's just another long term prisoner in my dungeon."

"Maybe you should talk with him. Sometimes you can be good at that."

"I dunno," I shook my head. "I stopped listening to his stories long ago. I just roll my eyes. But maybe he's got more to say, if I search for the real story..."

It hit me suddenly that just as I had hoped Josh might, some day, all on his own, take it into his head to apologize for cutting me out of his life so ruthlessly, maybe from my own father's point of view, there were times when I'd been a real asshole to him. Maybe I had some apologizing of my own still to do.

By this time the track had widened into a muddy road filled with porters and trekkers heading for the park exit. All hikers returning from the summit followed this one route down. The porters flew by, many of them at a run, anxious to drop their burdens at the final stop. Few of them bothered throwing a final *Jambo!* in our direction.

"Be cool, you crazy bananas!" Josh hollered as they passed.

I said, "You know, from a father's point of view there's a lot to celebrate when your kid turns into an adult. But it's also really sad to think, well, that's it. You're independent now. The cord is cut..."

"I think we're in a different place," said Josh. He spoke thoughtfully and deliberately. "I don't see you as a father figure any more. I still remember you as my dad who raised me. But the raising time is done. I don't expect you to continue to show me the ropes. I can figure out the ropes as I go. I guess having a father-son relationship is sort of like having a professional relationship. You were like my boss. You had your duties to raise me. I had duties to follow your rules to better myself. Now those duties are all gone. I'm setting my own rules, but I still remember that you were the one who got me on my way. So it's like getting together with the old boss after you've moved on. We have a more well-rounded understanding of each other because of the past. We've definitely seen each other at the best and worst. So it's good to talk about what's going on with our lives, discuss ideas, or just share the present moment. It feels more like a close, deep friendship, but with a lot of other things behind it."

We reached the bottom of the mountain.

It was disorienting to find concrete buildings, gardens, buses, billboards. A hundred porters milled about, repacking and loading gear on various vehicles. Fred brought us to the warden's post where we had to officially sign out of the park. We bought Kilimanjaro t-shirts from hawkers, then climbed on our bus back to Moshi. Sully was already on board, plus Fred, Frank, Benjamin, Nathanial, and all the rest of our crew. We clasped hands with them as we took our seats, and thanked them all one more time. The men were tired, but still laughing and joking in their local dialect. They were heading home to wives and children, or girlfriends and a night out on Moshi's bars. Some of them would be heading back up the mountain again in the morning.

I tallied up my tip money in my head for Fred to distribute when we got back to the hotel where I had stored my cash. Our tips would probably be more than their wages for the week. We had done our bit for Kilimanjaro's economy. Later I found out I had made a serious mistake here. On no account should the tip money be given to the guide, because they often keep far more than their share, or even take it all and give the porters nothing. Would Fred, the cheerful egalitarian, be so treacherous to his men? I could not imagine it. But savvy trekkers don't take the chance. They take the tip money with them and put it directly in the hands of each porter and guide individually at the end of the trail. I wish I had known better at the time.

Riding down through the foothills was like a long slide back to civilization. First we saw banana trees planted by the sides of houses, then rows of coffee plantations, schools, shops, traffic, billboards, Pepsi logos painted on concrete walls. A week ago, the memes of commerce, society and technology had sunk into the background, almost invisible to our eyes. Now it was almost painful to see nature transformed to serve our needs. My sense of alienation lasted until we returned to our hotel, and threw ourselves under hot showers.

Back at the Springlands Hotel we found Marita and Bastian. They were on their way to the coastal islands before heading home. A month later they sent us an email to tell us they got married. On our ride home to North America, we were delighted to discover Mike the Canadian was on our flight. He informed us that all of his group–Bryce with his brace, Vanessa, Gordon , and the four silver-haired New Zealanders–made it to the top of Kilimanjaro. We were thrilled.

"*Hakuna matata,*" Mike said.

"You know, Dad," said Josh thoughtfully on the flight home, "this Kilimanjaro trip is the first wilderness thing we've done together since I was 14. Thinking about it now, every other rafting and camping trip we've been on–this is getting to be metaphoric as hell–it was always you guiding me through the wilderness. You were like, 'Okay, Josh, now paddle, paddle, paddle. Now we're going to put up the tent.' You'd prep me on what to do. We were there together, but it was really as father and son, you taking care of me through it all. On Kilimanjaro it was different. I really did it. From the bottom up, I climbed it. Even when it was bad for me, I never felt like the kid, holding you back. You were never like, 'Poor Josh.' "

"Oh, I clamped down on my tongue a few times. I think the best moment for me was when you told me about your fall on the crater rim. At the time I thought, 'Oh my God, he fell and I didn't notice? What a lousy parent!' But then it hit me, 'No–he got himself up, shook off the guides, and walked to the peak.' I'm really proud of you, Josh. You pushed through so much pain. I respected you for keeping on going."

"Yeah, said Josh. "We really were just there for each other. Two guys individually climbing a mountain, together."

Epilogue

The Myth of Kilimanjaro

Once, there was the myth of Kilimanjaro,
A silver-topped mountain at the equator,
A green land when all East Africa was dry as bones.

We climbed, we conquered, we looked inside,
And in the ruins of that ancient ice,
We read the reckoning of our avaricious lives.

Now we make a vow to change our ways,
Before the silver turns to grey,
And the forests die.

Trekking Resources

Here's some valuable information for anyone seeking to climb Mount Kilimanjaro, beginning with some great organizations dedicated to the welfare of the porters, people and environment. In particular, I recommend checking out the website of the Kilimanjaro Porters Assistance Project for their list of partner companies which adhere to their standards for the fair and ethical treatment of porters.

I also urge those interested in climbing Kilimanjaro to read the Medical Commission of the UIAA brochure on travel at high altitude – the triple-starred reference below, which has crucial information on AMS. I can't express strongly enough how important it is to familiarize yourself well with the dangers of altitude sickness before climbing Kilimanjaro, and in selecting a company that you have confidence can handle an emergency. As Bastian said many times, people die, every year, climbing Kilimanjaro. The odds are remote, but they are real. Josh and I were fortunate. I was nowhere near as knowledgeable about AMS as I should have been, and I have heard a few very sad stories since our climb.

Kilimanjaro Porters Assistance Project

"Those who have climbed Mount Kilimanjaro know that the porters are the heart and soul of the trek. Without their hard work and strength climbers would not be able to fully experience the magnificence of Kilimanjaro. Porters are often impoverished Tanzanians who depend on this labor-intensive employment in order to feed themselves and their families. Porters can be underpaid and many climb without adequate clothing, footwear, or equipment. Porters are susceptible to altitude sickness, hypothermia and even death.

The Kilimanjaro Porters Assistance Project (KPAP) recognizes the value of the demanding labor these porters perform. Registered in January 2003, KPAP has been helping to improve the working conditions of the porters. Whether you are a climber, porter, guide, or managing a tour company, the Kilimanjaro Porters Assistance Project needs your help in ensuring fair treatment of all porters." For information: http://www.kiliporters.org

International Mountain Explorers Connection

"The International Mountain Explorers Connection (IMEC) is a U.S. 501(c)3 nonprofit organization founded in 1996 to promote responsible and sustainable connections between travelers and the people of developing mountain regions of the world. IMEC has a dual approach: working to benefit the local populations, primarily focusing on porters, while also working to educate visitors and link them to ways they can assist the local populations, particularly in demanding fair treatment for porters.

The International Mountain Explorers Connection created the Partnership for Responsible Travel Program to recognize those tour operators committed to fair treatment of the mountain crew. Acceptance as a Partner is based upon the climbing company's meeting IMEC's Guidelines for Proper Porter Treatment on Kilimanjaro through the monitoring activities performed by IMEC's local initiative, the Kilimanjaro Porters Assistance Project." For more information please visit: www.www.mountainexplorers.org/club/partnerprogram.htm

Medical Commission of the International Mountaineering and Climbing Federation (UIAA)

"The UIAA's medical commission provides a medical information service for mountaineers, including a page on medical risks associated with climbing Kilimanjaro and visiting Tanzania.

Their purpose is to give mountaineers reliable, practical advice and the most up to date recommendations on medical issues in the mountains. They function as a world-wide forum of doctors who are specialized in the different fields of mountain medicine. They collect, evaluate and discuss medical data from experts around the world and try to reach an international consensus on difficult issues of prevention and treatment of illness and injuries. They regularly publish recommendation papers which are available to everybody on the UIAA webpage. The UIAA's research includes issues of mountain equipment safety, diseases and altitude sickness, as well as Climate Change, sustainable development , and supporting mountain cultures around the world."

www.theuiaa.org

www.theuiaa.org/kilimanjaro.html

***www.theuiaa.org/upload_area/files/1/Travel_at_high_altitude_2009(0).pdf

Diamox: National Institute of Health

NIH has a valuable page on Diamox. Please research your options well for preparing for altitude sickness. http://www.ncbi.nlm.nih.gov/pubmedhealth/PMH0000766

General Trekking Information on Kilimanjaro:

www.tanzaniaparks.com/kili - The Kilimanjaro page on the Government of Tanzania's Parks website has good basic information, maps, and lots of useful links about the country.

http://kilitrekker.com - Blog that invites anyone to post their experiences and recommendations on Kilimanjaro.

www.Kilimanjaroclimbs.com – Information on climbing Kilimanjaro (sponsored by a company, but with great general information).

www.mtkilimanjarologue.com – Information website for climbing Kilimanjaro

www.tripadvisor.com/Tourism-g293750-Kilimanjaro_National _Park-Vacations - Reviews and recommendations from trekkers who have climbed Kilimanjaro.

www.zombiesonkilimanjaro.com. – You will find more information on my book's website, plus direct links to the information posted here, and more, so you don't have to type it all in to your computer.

Kilimanjaro Trekking Companies

You can only climb Kilimanjaro with a Tanzanian-based and registered trekking company. International outfitters must all subcontract through them. While booking directly through local companies may be cheaper, some of these have reputations for cutting corners and poor worker practices. Booking through a reputable international outfitter can help ensure you get an honest and ethical local company, as the international outfitters depend on high standards and customer satisfaction to keep their reputation. But there's no automatic guarantee of quality just because the company is international. You have to be diligent in your research to find an ethical, competent company. Take your time to compare several companies to find the one that best matches your own values, budget, and criteria for safety. (Consulting the KPAP website, above, can help you find outfits that have pledged to treat their porters fairly).

Here's a list of some Kilimanjaro outfitters to give you an idea of what's available. There are many other companies out there that did not respond to my invitation that you can also find online. Each of these companies provided their own description of their services (many of them offer African safaris as well). Please note that I am neither endorsing nor recommending any specific company, nor can I verify any of the information provided below. My intention in this section is simply to give you a good place to start your own search. (For phone numbers, below: in Tanzania, start with 255, with 44 in the UK and 1 in the US).

Adventures Within Reach

Adventures Within Reach offers all the routes on Kilimanjaro starting on any day. The 7-day Machame Route and the 6-day Rongai Route are our most popular routes, and about 25% of our climbers opt for the luxury trek upgrade. In 2011, we guided the oldest man to summit at 84 years old, and we had a woman climb the entire way barefooted! Add a safari and Zanzibar to your Kilimanjaro trek for the ultimate Tanzania experience.

www.AdventuresWithinReach.com

info@AdventuresWithinReach.com

1-303-325-3746, or 1-877-232-5836

African Environments

African Environments is owned and managed by outdoor enthusiasts with over 70 years of combined experience. We ensure the equipment is top grade, the guides are trained to the highest of level and the food is designed to be nutritious and balanced. We also ensure that our climbs are ethical: fair terms and conditions of our porters and making as little environmental impact as possible. Taking good care of people and the planet is the cornerstone of our ethos. We specialize in the wilderness routes of 'Kili' which offer a powerful experience, and which we helped develop. With a proven track record of outfitting thousands of climbs, we will get you to the top in style, making the climb a once in a lifetime experience on a physical, emotional and cultural level. We also have seasonal camps in the game parks of Northern Tanzania and offer incredible multi day walking safaris within the Serengeti National Park.

www.africanenvironments.com

adventure@africanenvironments.com

+255 784 700100

Africa Odyssey

Africa Odyssey specializes in tailor-made safaris to Tanzania and Zanzibar and include luxury climbs of Kilimanjaro.

www.africaodyssey.com

Africa Travel Resource

Since starting operations in 1999, Africa Travel Resource has provided Kilimanjaro treks to over 8,000 guests. Our company offers regular small group treks on Rongai (5 nights) and Shira (7 nights), and a 10 night North route that involves an almost complete circumnavigation of the mountain, taking in the virtually untrodden north side trails. We are very proud of our exemplary safety record. ATR is the only company able to offer the ALTOX Personal Oxygen System on Kilimanjaro which is proven to reduce the symptoms of altoxia (fast ascent altitude sickness). We are also great proponents of porter welfare, being one of very few operations which provides permanent employment, claiming that this is the only way to properly ensure quality of service and staff welfare. Our company has operational offices in Arusha, with bookings being handled by our offices in London, England and Grosse Pointe, USA.

www.africatravelresource.com/climbing-kilimanjaro
sales@africatravelresource.com
+44 1306 880770

Africa Wilderness Adventures

AWA is a full-service Tanzanian trekking company, based in Arusha, near Kilimanjaro. We will assist you with everything from planning the route to the right season of the year to getting the right gear to training for the challenge and ultimately to handle all the bookings and support for the climb itself. As a mountain, it is not be underestimated and our guides are extremely well qualified to cope with the extreme conditions and any emergencies that might occur. Where needed we provide oxygen bottles as well as a decompression chamber for the climb.

www.africanwildernessadventures.com
info@africanwildernessadventures.com
+255 754888457

Alpine Ascents International

Alpine Ascents International has been leading Kilimanjaro climbs for over twenty years renowned for our summit success and safety record. Each one of our climbs is led by an Alpine Ascents guide along with our hand-picked African staff.

www.AlpineAscents.com
gjanow@alpineascents.com
1-206-378-1927

Charity Challenge

Charity Challenge was formed over ten years ago by Jeremy Gane and Simon Albert to provide fund-raising treks for UK charities. The company brings great expertise in helping you plan your fund-raising climb of Kilimanjaro. You can join an open group and meet lots of other like-minded adventurers; or you can set up an exclusive group for your charity. We offer Rongai, 7-day and Lemosho, 8-day as a standard but we also operate other routes on request for charity groups. Our web site is packed with information to help you plan you climb to the roof of Africa.

www.CharityChallenge.com
Info@CharityChallenge.com
+44 (0)208-557-0000

Chui-Tours

We offer all routes to Kilimanjaro and offer all inclusive service. Clients can also book Safaris and beach holidays in Tanzania with us. We aim mostly at the German speaking market.

www.chui-tours.de
Tel +49 611 1824913

Deeper Africa

Stunning treks, less traveled routes. East African travel specialists Deeper Africa offers two treks up Kilimanjaro: Lemosho Route, an 8-day trek (10 days in country), and Machame Route, a 7-day trek (9 days in country). Trekkers can plan custom dates on either itinerary or choose from several group departure dates for Lemosho. Lemosho is a highly scenic, lesser-traveled route that offers additional time for acclimatization compared to other popular routes. Safety and quality are paramount along with ethical tourism, and Deeper Africa holds deep respect for the land and people of Tanzania. Guests are escorted by highly skilled and trained guides (including Wilderness First Responder certification and more than 100 summits) and porters using top equipment and safety gear. The climb is paced properly, and all meals are provided. Deeper Africa practices Leave No Trace camping techniques and is a Partner for Responsible Travel with Kilimanjaro Porters Assistance Project.

www.deeperafrica.com

info@deeperafrica.com

1-888-658-7102

Embark Adventures

Embark Adventures was founded on the slopes of Africa's highest peak. We take the road less traveled, the Lemosho to the Western Breach Route, which fewer than 10 percent of climbers follow. Embark boasts a climber's dream combination: very low foot traffic and a real focus on making the summit, not going fast. We also specialize in camping at the highest camp on Kilimanjaro, Crater Camp. We offer a high ratio of guides to clients with expert climbing expedition gear (mess tents, toilets, oxygen, gamo). And we believe in the places we travel, and invest money back into these communities by supporting local nongovernmental organizations such as the Kilimanjaro Porters Assistance Project in Tanzania.

www.embarkadventures.com.

Exodus

Exodus specializes in numerous itineraries from 6-8 days

including the Rongai, Lemosho and Northern Circuit routes, with extra days added to the standard itineraries to help aid acclimatisation.

www.exodus.co.uk/
sales@exodus.co.uk
0845 564 4754 or +44 2087 723 824

Explore

Explore offers three specialist treks to the summit of Kilimanjaro, using the two most beautiful and least busy routes – Lemosho and Rongai. All of Explore's treks include a generous amount of acclimatisation time, providing the best possible chance of reaching the summit at Uhuru Peak. Explore's Kilimanjaro treks are fully supported by a team of highly experienced porters, guides and cooks, whose welfare is imperative. Following the guidelines of both the International Porters Protection Group and the Kilimanjaro Porters Assistance Project, they are all paid a fair wage and have access to health care. All are given the correct equipment to work with and do not carry excessive loads.

www.explore.co.uk / 0844 499 0901 from the UK
www.exploreworldwide.com / 1 800 715 1746/ USA.

Explore Travel AS

Marit and Vidar, the owners of Explore Travel AS have been organising active trips since 1996. Kilimanjaro has been and will be one of the favourite trips for Norwegians! Most of our clients choose to hike Rongai, Marangu and Machame routes. Mainly we are doing tours for groups, Norwegian tour leaders always follow the groups. As a give-back to Tanzania we support schools and children home in Marangu area.

www.exploretravel.no

Gane and Marshall

Gane and Marshall have operated Kilimanjaro climbs for over 20 years. They can offer you the chance to try any route on the mountain and you can also join open groups to keep your costs down. When you choose a climb operator you will hopefully want to consider the advice you will receive about routes best suited to you, you will want to know about the climate, the clothing and equipment, the conditions on the mountain. Gane and Marshall climbs are comprehensively documented and each climber receives a very full and useful Confirmation Pack at the time of booking and Travel Pack just before setting out to Tanzania. The climbs are managed by Jeremy Gane, who has climbed the mountain 21 times. He was appointed to look after the very famous March 2009 Red Nose Day celebrity climb for Comic Relief. Jeremy will look after you from the moment you begin your enquiry to the time of your climb.

www.GaneandMarshall.com

Jeremy@GaneandMarshall.com

+44 (0)1822-600-600, Mobile:07815-033-868

Good Earth Tours

Since 1995, Good Earth Tours offers a wide range of outdoor and wildlife adventures in the world famous Serengeti, Masai Mara and Kilimanjaro Parks as well as several other less traveled parks throughout East Africa. For Kilimanjaro treks, the company offers 6 different routes to suit your level of fitness and travel preferences. Our professionally certified guides undergo rigorous training through Trailmed - an internationally recognized wilderness safety training organization. Rates are competitive and clients can include medical equipment such as hyperbaric chamber, emergency oxygen and pulse oximeter as needed. Good Earth Tours is committed to ethical treatment of porters (proud member of KPAP) and a portion of our proceeds is donated to local Tanzania communities including non profits, orphanages and primary/secondary schools.

www.goodearthtours.com

The Heritage Safari Company

We specialize in private climbs. Each climb is customized to our clients' needs. We offer different level of services on Lemosho, Machame and Rongai route, from standard to luxury specifications.

The Heritage Safari Company is member of " Kilimanjaro porters assistance project".

www.heritagesafaris.com/

info@heritagesafaris.com

778-340 1999, 1- 888 301 1713

Hoopoe Safaris

We are unique in that very few companies, if any, actually operate their own climbs on Mt Kenya, Mt Meru and Kilimanjaro. We have been operating Kilimanjaro, Mt Kenya and Mt Meru climbs for well over a decade. Over time our specification has always been among the very highest. In terms of companies operating on Kilimanjaro we excel in a number of areas: Ethics, Porters Welfare, Guide and Staff Training, Equipment used for clients and staff, First Aid training to the highest levels, Flying Doctors Membership for all. We are members of the Kilimanjaro Porters Assistance Project (KPIP), the Africa Travel & Tourism Associations (ATTA), and The Tanzanian Association of Tour Operators (TATO). For further information about the high quality of our treks, please read Bradt Guides, the Lonely Planet Guide, or Trip Advisor.

www.hoopoe.com

hoopoeuk@aol.com

IntoAfrica

IntoAfrica UK Ltd runs mountain treks and safaris in Tanzania and Kenya based on the principles of fair trade. We will not appeal to seekers of the "luxury-lodge colonial" experience, but rather those seeking a genuine appreciation of Africa and its peoples. We employ qualified mountain guides, wildlife experts and local guides who are effective communicators - not simply there to walk ahead of you up the track. They know about the plants, wildlife, history and folklore of the country, making your holiday experiences so much richer. Our direct support for schools, community projects and rights campaigns, over and above our employment of only local staff on a profit sharing scheme, contributes to the long term sustainability of communities managing their own natural resources.

www.intoafrica.co.uk

enquiry@intoafrica.co.uk

+44 (0)114 255 5610

Jipe Trekking and Safaris

Our specialty is custom and tailor-made mountain climbing and safaris in Tanzania. We assure you a friendly, knowledgeable and personalized service and attention to the smallest details. We treat each booking as a private departure regardless of how many persons are booked together, 1 or 10+. We may have several trekking departures on the same route on the same day and you can choose to trek together or separately. As you are all independent groups, with your own guide and cook you are independent of each other and your bid to get to the summit will not be influenced by the weakness of others. We specialize in: Mount climbing, wildlife safaris, cultural tours, Day trips, Zanzibar Beach tours and Volunteer placements.

info@jipetrekkingandsafaris.com

www.jipetrekkingandsafaris.com

KE Adventure Travel

Operating since 1984, KE Adventure Travel specialises in-group and private tours on all the main Kilimanjaro routes, including the Lemosho/Shira; Rongai and Machame routes. With a extra time allowed for acclimatisation, recognised by the Kilimanjaro

Porter Assistance Group and fully bonded with ABTA, and holders of an ATOL license means you can book your climb with complete confidence.

www.keadventure.com

Kilimanjaro Expeditions

At Kilimanjaro Expeditions we pride ourselves on a high quality climbing experience for our clients, as well as on our company's ethics. First, we ensure that our porters are paid fairly and they have the appropriate gear and equipment to endure the environments of Kilimanjaro. We also do everything we can to reduce our environmental impact by practicing leave no trace standards while we are on the mountain, as well as operating a 100 percent green energy and paper-free office when we are not.

www.kilimanjaroexpeditions.com

Maasai Wanderings

We offer Mid Range to High end treks on Kilimanjaro - committed to our fair-traded ethics for all.

www.maasaiwanderings.com or www.mwtreks.com

Macs Adventure

Macs Adventure is a small, energetic company with a commitment to responsible travel and to the delivery of outstanding customer service. We specialise in private high quality Kilimanjaro climbs on the Machame, Lemosho & Rongai routes for couples and small pre-formed groups. Our specialists, who have all summited Kilimanjaro, will help you to choose the best route and tailor the trip to your requirements, giving you the highest chance of success on Kilimanjaro.

www.macsadventure.com

info@macsadvenure.com

+44 (0)141 530 8886

Mountain and River Activities Ltd.

Mountain and River Activities Ltd have been organising trips to Kilimanjaro since 1995 specialising in the Machame and Rongai routes. We run bespoke treks for charities, and other groups, also individuals are more than welcome. To lessen the work load on porters we allocate three porters per client. We are a member of IMEC and committed to the ethical treatment of porters on Kilimanjaro.

www.mountainandriveractivities.co.uk
info@mountainandriveractivities.co.uk
+44 01639711690

Mountain Madness

Mountain Madness climbs the Western Breach via the Shira Plateau, a route pioneered by company founders Scott Fischer and Wesley Krause in the early 1980s. This seldom-traveled route is considered by many the best non-technical route on the mountain. Our summit day is only a 1-2 hour hike from our high camp. Participants enjoy our private camps in Arusha National Park before the climb and in the Ngorongoro and Serengeti while on safari. Mountain Madness has more than 25-year's experience on the mountain and on safari.

www.mountainmadness.com
1-800-328-5925 or 1-206-937-8389

Peak Planet

Peak Planet is one of the few specialist companies organizing high quality group and private climbs on Mount Kilimanjaro's most popular routes. We have an established reputation as a solid, safe, and dependable operator. We pledge a strict standard of service on all of our climbs, including: professional local guides; high guide to client ratio; team-oriented support staff; four-season mountain tents; dining tents with table and chairs; fresh, healthy, nutritious food; purified drinking water; sanitary toilet tents; crisis management and safety procedures; fair and ethical treatment of porters; environmentally responsible trekking.

www.PeakPlanet.com

info@peakplanet.com

1-480-463-4058

Private Kilimanjaro

Private Kilimanjaro is a specialist operator dedicated to helping you climb Kilimanjaro safely, whether it is a group or private climb or a charity challenge. To give you the very best chance of a successful Kilimanjaro climb we directly control every aspect of your climb ourselves. We choose the best guides, buy the very best kit available and carefully plan all the food menus. We are experts in arranging custom made, bespoke Kilimanjaro climbs with the extras to make your trip really special. Champagne at the summit, a birthday cake carried to the summit, candlelit dinner- whatever you might like we can arrange. What allows us to do this, and what differentiates us from most companies offering Kilimanjaro climbs, is that we are operators not agents. We never sub-contract your safety and enjoyment to someone else. If you book with us you climb Kilimanjaro with us.

www.privatekilimanjaro.com

+44 115 714 1174 or +1-415-513-1174

Snowcap Limited

Snowcap limited is a tour company based in Moshi - Kilimanjaro - Tanzania. The company was established in 1991 and we do organise all the mountain routes to Kilimanjaro but we are more specialised on the Nalemoru route - the Rongai route as other names. Snowcap is committed to treatment of porters and also adhere to its standards. We are partners for responsible travel with KPAP - Kilimanjaro porters assistance project and with IMEC - International mountain explorers connection. Snowcap also owns Snowcap Cottages, located 500 metres to the Rongai - Nalemoru starting point gate. Clients can stay for overnight at the cottages and acclimatise before ascent.

www.snowcap.co.tz

snowcap@kilinet.co.tz

+255-2754826 / 2750888

Summit Expeditions and Nomadic Experience

Summit Expeditions & Nomadic Experience (SENE), located in Moshi, Tanzania, offers Kilimanjaro treks, custom private safaris, exciting bicycle and running adventures, as well as Zanzibar trips. What makes SENE distinct is our Mbahe Farm, a unique cultural experience and SENE's private cottages for adventurers located on the slopes of Kilimanjaro. Simon Mtuy, SENE owner and world-record holder for fastest unsupported ascent-descent of Kilimanjaro continues to carry out his vision of a sustainable, Tanzanian-owned and operated adventure outfitter that promotes the beauty of Tanzania while contributing to the well-being of its people and environment. Karibu!

www.nomadicexperience.com/trips-kili

info@nomadicexperience.com

1-866-417-7661

Tanzania Tours, Denmark

Specialists in the Danish market, for all routes on Kili. Can be combined with safari or leisure on Zanzibar.

www.tanzaniatours.dk

0045 61 70 16 10

Tusker Trail

Tusker Trail is one of the oldest Kilimanjaro climbing companies. The company founder and owner, Eddie Frank, ran Tusker's first climb in 1977. As a result of Tusker's unique world-class guide training program, and its attention to trip details, the quality of its climbs is used as a benchmark for most other climbing companies.

www.tusker.com

Ultimate Kilimanjaro

We are a US-based tour operator specializing in safe, high quality, fully supported, small party climbs on Mount Kilimanjaro at reasonable rates. We offer weekly group treks on Lemosho, Machame and Rongai during the dry season and private, custom climbs on all routes year round. Our local guides are professional and very experienced, with most having more than 100 successful summits. All guides are certified by the park, and have extensive training in first aid, altitude sickness prevention and treatment, and mountain rescue. Our porters are paid a fair wage, properly clothed and equipped, fed nutritious meals and carry limited loads. Over 500 people from all over the world climb with us annually. We have guided literally thousands of climbers to the top of Kilimanjaro.

www.ultimatekilimanjaro.com

Wild Frontiers

Wild Frontiers has been at the forefront of trekking and mountaineering holidays since 1991. We offer a range of hiking trips to suit all levels of ability and fitness in Africa, Asia and South America. Our friendly staff members have first-hand knowledge of most of the hiking routes, and offer in-depth advice on all aspects of your trip. We are active members of the International Porters Protection Group. Our Responsible Tourism Ethic is highlighted in the fact that we are the only South African company complying with international guidelines in the care of our staff, porters and the environment. Wild Frontiers offer regular departures for individuals or groups. We will discuss, in detail with you, the different routes available, as well as the preparation required for such a trip. We are also the proud organizers of the annual Kilimanjaro Marathon event at the base of Kilimanjaro.

www.wildfrontiers.com, www.kilimanjaromarathon.com

reservations@wildfrontiers.com

+27 (0) 87 941 3892 1 +27 (0) 72 927 7529

Wilderness Travel

We've perfected the climb via the Shira-Western Breach Route, an incredibly beautiful trail on Kili's remote southwest flank that showcases its magnificent glaciation and five ecological zones. We pioneered this route, and it's the ultimate way to climb Kili. A full seven days on the ascent provide us with maximum acclimatization, shorter hiking days, and the greatest chance of summit success. Our Kili guides are legendary and they make the climb an unforgettable experience. We recommend our stunning safari in the Ngorongoro Crater and the great plains of the Serengeti as your post-climb reward.

www.wildernesstravel.com/trip/tanzania/serengeti-safari-kilimanjaro-climb

Climate Change and Environment on Kilimanjaro

While there are excellent scientific articles about ongoing research on the rapidly shrinking glaciers, online search engines kick up a deluge of misinformation when one enters "Kilimanjaro Climate Change." I've read through many of these articles written by Climate Change deniers. I notice they pick and choose data in order to discredit the idea that Climate Change as a key driver in accelerating the disappearance of Kilimanjaro's glaciers. I believe there is a political agenda at work here that is neither driven nor informed by science. Indeed, a lot more research needs to be done on Kilimanjaro. As this book labors to make clear, the way of science is to doubt and question. And there is such a large body of factual evidence and research that supports human-caused global warming that over a hundred national and international scientific bodies have written declarations, signed by their members, asserting this reality. So, while we continue to gather this information to better understand what is happening to our home, I believe we owe it to our children and all other living creatures, to stop emitting greenhouse gases that we do know cause planetary warming. For your reference:

Here's the 2009 article I quoted from Nature Magazine:
www.nature.com/nature/journal/v462/n7270/full/462140d.html

Here is the article of the original findings the Kilimanjaro research team published in the Proceedings of the national Academy of Sciences, November 2009:
www.ncbi.nlm.nih.gov/pmc/articles/PMC2771743/

Here's a CNN report on the same research:
http://articles.cnn.com/2009-11-02/tech/kilimanjaro.glaciers

_1_glaciers-mount-kilimanjaro-lonnie-thompson?_s=PM:TECH

Here's a list of all the scientific bodies who have signed declarations attesting to the reality of human-caused Climate Change: http://en.wikipedia.org/wiki/Scientific_opinion_on_climate_change#Statements_by_concurring_organizations:

Here's the website of the UN's International Panel on Climate Change:
http://www.ipcc.ch/

Here's WWF's Climate Change page. It's a great place to get informed and get involved: http://www.worldwildlife.org/climate

About the Author

Tim Ward is the author of six books, including the best-selling *What the Buddha Never Taught* and *Savage Breast: One Man's Search for the Goddess*. His travel stories have appeared in 13 anthologies, including *Traveler's Tales Best Travel Writing 2006, 2010, 2011 and 2012*. Tim is also the publisher of Changemakers Books (an imprint of John Hunt Publishing). He also co-owns Intermedia Communications Training with Teresa Erickson, his wife and business partner. They live in Maryland

For more information, to see photos and videos of Kilimanjaro, read more articles about the mountain, people and environment, or to contact Tim Ward, please visit

www.zombiesonkilimanjaro.com
www.timwardsbooks.com
www.changemakers-books.com
www.intermediacommunicationstraining.com

**CHANGEMAKERS
BOOKS**

Changemakers publishes books for individuals committed to transforming their lives and transforming the world. Our readers seek to become positive, powerful agents of change. Changemakers books inform, inspire, and provide practical wisdom and skills to empower us to create the next chapter of humanity's future.
Please visit our website at www.changemakers-books.com